Bryan Tyson

A Ray of Light

A Treatise on the Sectional Troubles, Religiously and Morally Considered

Bryan Tyson

A Ray of Light
A Treatise on the Sectional Troubles, Religiously and Morally Considered

ISBN/EAN: 9783337254070

Printed in Europe, USA, Canada, Australia, Japan

Cover: Foto ©Lupo / pixelio.de

More available books at **www.hansebooks.com**

A RAY OF LIGHT;

OR,

A TREATISE ON THE SECTIONAL TROUBLES,

RELIGIOUSLY AND MORALLY CONSIDERED.

BY

BRYAN TYSON.

BROWER'S MILLS, N. C.
PUBLISHED BY THE AUTHOR
1862.

PREFACE.

My object in writing this little book is that we may soon see these sectional troubles, that threaten to destroy our once happy country speedily settled, and without the further spilling of blood.

I do not claim perfect originality for this work. I am thus indebted to Messrs. A. H. Stevens of Georgia and Edward Everett of Massachusetts for valuable extracts from their writings. I am also indebted to that excellent paper, the Fayetteville Observer, for valuable extracts, which are not credited, and to many other sources. My reasons for doing so are, that I have changed some of them from their original text and they can't therefore, in their present shape be properly credited to their respective sources, and another is that by doing so the thread of the discourse would be broken and their usefulness thus probably impaired. I have therefore endeavored to give them in as connected a link as possible.

This little book, owing to the shortness of time since I first conceived the idea of writing it, together with my own inability, is doubtless defective in many particulars, but owing to circumstances I consider it best to put it to press immediately, rather than to keep it off for a longer time for the purpose of making such of these corrections as I might be able to do. With these remarks I herewith submit the following pages to a careful perusal of the reader.

A RAY OF LIGHT,

OR, A TREATIES ON THE SECTIONAL TROUBLES,

Religiously and morally considered.

CHAPTER I.

THE SECTIONAL TROUBLES.

Dear Friends:—I, having a universal desire for the welfare of my fellow man, am induced to write the following, and will feel amply compensated for my trouble in doing so, should it tend, even to a small degree, to alleviate their sufferings and better their condition—to stop the torrents of blood that now flow, or that occasionally flows, or that that is within their veins giving life and vigor to the system, destined soon to flow:—this parts soul and body, and sends a soul to everlasting happiness or everlasting woe. Man is a compound being taking on two states of existence, the one in this world, at longest, is but short, the one in the next has eternity for its measure. He is there to live a miserable or happy creature forever and ever. It should be the great business of this life to prepare for the next. The time of our probation here is short enough to prepare for this great change, without inventing machines and all manner of warlike instruments with which to shorten the days of our fellow man, sending them into a boundless eternity without one moment's warning, creating orphans and widows and an amount of misery that can never be told.

Wars then are a great evil and are generally a dreadful scourge to any nation that engages therein. The victor is generally loser. The good and the bad suffer together. Why is it that enlightened man thus becomes arrayed with hostile intent against his fellow man? I think it must be owing to the depravity and wickedness of human nature. I will venture to say that there never was a war but some one was in fault. By some party or some individuals acting differently it might have been avoided. Yes, I think I can safely say that by all acting according to the golden rule, " As ye would that others should do unto you, do ye likewise unto them," for this is the law and the prophets, that there would be no wars. It is I think by wrong men being in power that wars are generally brought about—men who are not willing to give and take, but are determined to have every thing their own way, let the consequences be as they may. I will illustrate this a little by a piece on walking the streets.

Have you ever walked through the crowded streets of a great city? We will say for instance that it is Broadway, New York. What shoals of people pouring in from opposite quarters like torrents meeting in a narrow valley! You would imagine it impossible for them all to get through, yet all pass on their way without stop or molestation. Were each man to proceed exactly in the same line in which he set out, he could not move many paces without encountering another full in his track. They would strike against each other, fall back, push forward again, and block up the way for themselves and those after them, and thus throw the whole street into confusion.

All this is avoided by every man yielding a little.

Instead of advancing square, stiff, with arms stuck out, every one who knows how to walk the streets glides along, his arms close, flexible, his track gently winding, leaving now a few inches on this side, now a few on that, so as to pass and be passed without scarcely touching in the smallest possible space. He pushes no one into the kennel nor goes into it himself. By mutual accommodation the path, though narrow, holds them all.

Like this is the march of life.

In our progress through the world a thousand things stand continually in our way. Some people meet us full in the face with opposite opinions and inclinations. Some stand before us in our pursuit of pleasure or interest, and others follow close upon our heels. Now we ought in the first place to consider, *that the road is as free for one as for another*; and therefore we have no right to expect that persons should go out of their way to accommodate us any more than we out of ours to accommodate them.

Then if we do not mutually yield and accommodate, we may expect to be continually getting in difficulties that might have been worn off by this balm of peace—mutual accommodation.

We should remember what Solomon says:

"A soft answer turneth away wrath, but grievous words stir up confusion."

And again.

"By long forbearance is a prince persuaded and a soft tongue breaketh the bone."

We should also not be too ready to reply to what we may hear said about us.

By an observance of these rules and by not being too hasty to resent supposed injuries, many difficulties might be killed off at the start, as it were, which afterwards grow into something very serious. But begin to work with them, one evil word calleth for another, and the farther you go the worse things get to be, and they thus soon get to be almost past healing.

It is like pulling at a splinter on a cross grained piece of timber. The more you strip it up the deeper it runs into the timber until it runs quite across the piece. Instead of doing this, smoothe it down, and it will all soon be right.

So in life we meet up with many cross grained people, who may do many things not right, but, instead of creating difficulties with them out of trivial matters, make the necessary allawances for human nature and pass on.

Thomas Jefferson was said to be a man of such perfect control over himself that he was but rarely if ever known to get out of humor. If any one were to try to offend him, he would turn it upon him in some mild way so as to make him his friend rather than his enemy. What a pity it is that such a spirit does not more generally pervade the bosom of man.

We should recollect that our Heavenly Father is slow to anger, and of much forbearance towards us. Had he dealt with us as he might in justice have done, long ere this we might have ridden the pale horse into the valley and shadow of death, and there have been lifting our fruitless cries for mercy, where neither mercy nor hope could ever have reached us. But we are yet the spared monuments of his meccy. Therefore, it becometh us to act with much forbearance towards our fellow man.

A timely observance of these inestimable rules would, I think, have kept us out of our present difficulties.

Our once happy country is now involved in a terrific

civil strife, such probably as has not been since the creation of the world.

After looking at some of the causes of this war, I will then give my opinion as to what I think of the general issue, and what I think, under the trying times, we had best do.

This business has been brooding in Congress for a great while. Ambitious men, and men of opposite opinions and inclinations, have frequently got up dissensions there, as in the caning affair of Brooks of South Carolina and Sumner of Massachusetts. There was also, some years ago, a Congressman from Californa, who shot a waiter in Willard's hotel. There has also at times been serious opposition made to the South in recovering their fugitive slaves, sometimes resulting even in bloodshed.

There was also, the affair of John Brown & Co. at Harper's Ferry. I do not wish to be understood as arguing the case in favor of these wicked men in making an unprovoked attack upon their brethren of the South and inciting their slaves to insurrection. But I do think had the South have been more lenient upon that occasion that it would have had a very great bearing upon our present troubles. Not but they deserved death, they doubtless did. But as the greater part of their number had been either killed or wounded, I think it was a sufficient warning to the balance, and that they, the surviving ones, could with all safety to the commonwealth have been spared at least their lives. I think, had they been pardoned upon their giving good and ample bond for their better behavior in future, that it would have had an excellent effect in reconciling the two sections. The good effect that such a course would as I believe, have had in reconciling the two sections, is my main reason for arguing that they should not have been hanged.

These Northern fanatics had learned at least two important lessons by this affair, which would probably have been of benefit to them and to us for generations to come. One was their inability to accomplish anything by such an undertaking, and the other, and by far the most important lesson that they learned was, that our servants were by no means so much disaffected as they had supposed, and would therefore, not join the North in a crusade against the South to gain their liberties, not even when opportunity offered. Having learned these things, I don't suppose they would hardly ever have tried the thing over again.

It therefore, think a better plan than hanging these men would have been to have liberated them, and even have had a good minister to pray for them on their departure, and tell them any time they wished to try the like, to come on again. As they appeared to be a party of fanatics or mad men, let us of the South, as a great and forgiving people, have shown that we could be satisfied without desiring their blood. Such a course as this, I think, would have made the people of the North ashamed of themselves, and they would not therefore, have tried the like soon again if ever. Such a course as this, I think, would have united the North and South in perpetual bonds. Another reason that I have for arguing that these men should not have been hung is, that the main persons at the North concerned in this affair, and principal in bringing it about, were not engaged in active service, and therefore escaped with impunity, I think those actively engaged had already suffered enough, or at least enough to do, and if we could then have managed it in such a way as to have made the balance (instigators) ashamed of themselves, I think it would, under the circumstances, have been the best course that we could have pursued.

So strongly was I impressed that there was something ominous in this affair, that I wrote to Governor Wise desiring that they should not be hung. I also stated to him that as they appeared to be a party of fanatics or madmen, and having by this experiment learned that our servants were by no means so much disaffected as they had supposed, and that they could not, therefore, accomplish anything by such an undertaking, that by pardoning them, I thought it might eventually result as an advantage in uniting the two sections and killing out the strong sectional feeling.

But it appeared to have no effect, but in doing this, I was discharging what I conceived to be my duty and that was all that I could do.

In Congress some years ago, they were, I believe, about too months electing a Speaker of the House. These things all taken together no doubt, ten led to inflame their respective sections, and thus make the breach between the two sections greater, and I think, also goes to prove conclusively that we had not the right men in power. Men who wish to serve their country, should not go to Congress armed with Bowie knives, canes and pistols, ready to resort to violence even upon trivial matters. They should, also, I think, be men that are willing to give and take.

CHAPTER II.

SECESSION OF SOUTH CAROLINA.

The immediate case of our difficulties and of the Southern States seceding, was the election of Abraham Lincoln to the Presidency of the United States. It is true, there were other causes, but this is the one that gave action to the others. South Carolina was the first to secede. Her Convention passed the ordinance of secession by a unanimous vote of 169, all the members voting, on December 20th, 1860. Florida, Georgia, Alabama, Mississippi, Louisana and Texas soon followed, making seven in all. The balance of the slave States would, in all probability, have remained in the Union as they were for some time to come, had it not been for the affair growing out of the capture of Fort Sumpter, and the call of the President soon after for 75,000 additional troops.

The field here opens far and wide. It will be impossible for me to give the subject anything like a thorough investigation, but I will endeavor to glance at some of the leading items. In the first place, I will remark that I do not look upon secession as the immediate cause of the war, or at least not so much so as some of the subsequent acts, for the following reasons. The States evidently formed the Union, and I think, each state should have the right to secede at pleasure. We will say that thirteen persons form a copartnership for the purpose of transacting any business whatever, and subsequently take in others upon the same footing to the amount of thirty two in all. After trading together for a number of years, and growing pretty strong, some one, two or a half dozen of these persons wish to withdraw and set up business for themselves. No one I presume will deny their having a perfect right to do so. Even so with the states. It is the people of the states that compose the states, and they have the same right, I think to withdraw and set up for themselves, as though there were but thirteen individuals. But in this case, it should, I think, always be submitted to a popular vote of the people. But I do not say that it is best thus to secede and split up, but rather the reverse, because in union there is strength. Better if possible allay the difficulties and time will soon make all right again.

Then, as stated before, I look upon the acts that were committed after the seceding of the states as having more to do in bringing on the war than I do upon secession itself.

A subject fraught with so much importance as secession is, should always, I think, be left to a popular vote of the people, for fear that the minority might rule, and a state be declared out of the union by these Conventions, when a majority of the farmers and mechanics— the bone and and the sinew of the country, and the men who have the most of the fighting to do, if there is any done, are for peace and union. I therefore, think they should have a say-so in the matter. The people that are good enough to fight, I think should also be good enough to vote upon a subject of so very great importance. Let the question be put fairly to the people at the polls, and let them vote fairly upon it, for or against secession. If there be a majority against secession, let them remain in the Union, but if a majority in favor of secession, I think they should be allowed to depart in peace. Let the majority rule, and be certain you have the majority.

I will illustrate this idea by reference to the last Presidential election.

Lincoln was constitutionally elected, receiving 180 electorial votes, whilst the other three candidates received jointly but 123, but at the same time these three candidates received more votes than Lincoln did by 1,001,-248. So had the election have depended on the popular vote, the election would have been thrown in the House, and in all probability Mr. Lincoln would have been defeated.

Even so, probably with some of the States that have been passed out of the Union unanimously by Conventions, the result might have been different, had the people have voted directly on it, for or against secession at the *ballot box*. But even if the result had been the same, the people are the sovereign power and should, therefore, have spoken directly upon it. A State being carried out of the Union, even unanimously by a Convention, is not always conclusive evidence that even a majority of her constitutional voters are in favor of it.

If a man is to be tried for his life for murder, we will say it is necessary before convicting him, that his guilt be established beyond a shadow of doubt, lest an innocent man should suffer. Even so in this case. Before a State secedes, I think it should be established beyond a shadow of doubt, that a majority of her constitutional voters are in favor of taking such a step, and this can only be known by deciding it at the *ballot box*.

When South Carolina seceded it is said that only 10,000 votes were cast for the members of the Convention that passed her out of the Union—10,000 out of over 60,000. See 1. (Appendix.)

Although South Carolina was passed out of the Union unanimously by her Convention, there is no certainty that there was even a majority of her constitutional voters in favor of secession. The fact is, it seems as it might have been otherwise.

In 1850 we had a great crisis among us, resultiug, I believe, mainly from the repeal of the Missouri Compromise. There were then many persons among us disirous of disrupting every tie and going immediately out of the Union. South Carolina always foremost in such things, made the attempt to go out, but her people voted upon it and put it down. And who can tell but the same would have been the result of 1860, had her people have had an opportunity of voting directly upon it. But her politicians, and no doubt wisely too for their schemes, kept this thing away from them, and it is therefore left in doubt to this day, whether or not the majority ruled. Soon after the John Brown raid, South Carolina sent Commissioners to Virginia in order to bring on general secession.

The people of our own State have always been rampant about the rights of the people, such as free suffrage, ad valorum, &c., and great hobbies have been made of these things. But upon a subject I trow of the most importance that has been before the American people since the days of the revolution or the war of 1812, they were not permitted to speake directly upon it. These things, I think they ought to have done and not to have left the others undone.

When our Legislature resolved to call a Convention they passed an act that each and every Ordinance passed by this Convention should be submitted to the people for ratification or rejection before it should become a law. See 2.

That would, in my opinion, have been doing things up in the right way. If after the Convention had passed the Ordinance of secession it had then been submitted to the people to ratify or reject at the polls, and they had ratified it, I don't think any nation upon earth should have had any right to have interfered therewith. But the Convention at length passed the Ordinance of secession (20th May,) and it was not submitted to the people for ratification or rejection according to the act prescribed for the Convention, that was voted for on the 28th of Febuary, 1861. Why was this not done ? Who is responsible?

But I will here remark that the members of the Convention voted for on the 28th of Febuary, did not assemble from the fact that a majority of the people voted "no Convention." But why did not this same act apply to the Convention that was subsequently convened and passed the Ordinance of Secession ? I can't see why it should not have applied in the last case as well as the first.

I will here remark that the Constitution of the United States was, I believe, submitted to the people for ratification or rejection at the polls. So why was not the Constitution of the Confederate States submitted in the same way? This thing was discussed in the Confederate Congress, but a gentleman from Alabama opposed it, and the thing fell through. I look upon this though as of much less importance than I do upon the Ordinance of Secession. I think by all means, the people of the seceding States should have voted directly on that.

CHAPTER III.

TAKING OF FORT SUMPTER.

The Secession of South Carolina as has been before stated, took place on the 20th December, 1860.

Six other States mentioned soon followed. They soon leagued together and erected a Provisional Government at Montgomery, Alabama, and elected Jefferson Davis of Mississippi, President and A. H. Stephens, of Georgia, Vice President. Soon after this, the authorities of the Southern Confederacy sent Commissioners to Washington to treat respecting the forts, public property, &c. The authorities at Washington refused to receive them in their official capacity, but expressed defference for them as gentlemen, See 3. So their mission availed them nothing, and they returned from whence they came, after first having expressed the conviction that they deemed war inevitable. In the mean time, the authorities of South Carolina demanded Fort Sumpter of the Federal Government, Major Anderson Commanding. It seems that the Federal Government would have given up this Fort without any difficulty, had not the Southern authorities demanded a regular surrender of the fort. See 4, 5, 6, 7.

Col. Lamon, an agent of the Federal Government was then, I believe, sent to Charleston. He informed Governor Pickens, that he was authorized to make arrangements for the withdrawal of the Federal troops from sumpter, and proposed a vessel of war as the best means of effecting this. This was refused. See Cause and Contrast, page 171, and appendix 8.

The authorities at Washington then sent a Mr. Fox, who declared that his mission was entirely pacific and wished to be permitted to visit Fort Sumpter. Through the intervention of Captain Hartstene, his wish was complied with. But intercepted dispatches disclosed the fact that whilst at Fort Sumpter he concocted a plan for supplying the Fort by force. From what I can find out it was a plan simply for supplying the Fort with provisions, and I think, was not for the forcible reinforcement of the Fort, as is said in Cause and Contrast, page 172. And farther, this plan was not, I don't think concocted with the Federal Government previous to Mr. Fox's leaving Washington, as is held out by the same author and upon the same page, but it seems to have been a plan concocted at Fort Sumpter, between Mr. Fox and the authorities of the Fort, and which plan was subsequently adopted by the Government at Washington. See Western Sentinel of April 26th. My reason for thus speaking, is, that I desire to speak nothing but what is true, if I know it, and if I see any thing wrongly stated, I wish to correct it, let it be on which side it may. It is the only fair way to come at things.

The authorities at Washington, I believe, next sent Lieut. Talbot and a Mr. R. S. Chew, to inform the authorities at Charleston that Fort Sumpter would be provisioned (the supplies were cut off the 7th of April) peaceable if practicable—forcibly if necessary. It seems there was no intention to reinforce the fort but simply to supply it with provisions.

The following from the Brother Jonathan of 20th April, 1861, may also throw some light on the subject: "Perhaps too, the publication of the government plan by which means the Charlestonians were fully put on their guard, had something to do with the delay. The army and navy officers entrusted with the fitting out of the expedition from New

York, on Saturday, Sunday and Monday last kept their secret well. No man could find out a word from them. But Wednesday morning—long before the expedition reached, or could reach Charleston—the New York Tribune revealed the whole plan. It gave the name of the commander, Lieut. Col. Harvey Brown, of the 2nd artillery, and on Thursday it reported and enlarged upon the plans, &c.

On Thursday, therefore, Gen. Beuregard, the commander in chief of the forces of the "Southern Confederacy," demanded the evacuation of Fort Sumter. Major Anderson replied that he should surrender, if not reinforced, when his supplies were exhausted. His exact language was: "I regret that my sense of honor and my obligations to my government prevent my compliance," and added, "Probably I will await the first shot, and if you do not batter us to peices we shall be starved out in a few days."

From the above it would seem that General Beauregard was hurried to make his demand from the fact that a fleet was on its way from New York to supply the fort.

The authorities concerned failing to agree as to the terms of surrender, &c., Gen. Beauregard opened fire on the fort on Friday morning, the 12th of April, at half past 4 o'clock.

The firing continued all that day and until about 12 o'clock at night. It was resumed at an early hour next morning, and continued until 2 o'clock, P. M., when the fort surrendered, with no loss on either side except the wounding of a few by the explosion of one of Maj. Anderson's guns wh 1st saluting his flag.

Here I conceive, is the turning point as to the justification of this war. If the national honor and exigencies of the case rendered it necessary to fire upon and capture the fort, and induct civil war at that time, then was the act justifiable; otherwise, it is rendered more doubtful. It appears though that certain of our public men at that time would not do anything towards bringing about a reconciliation so as to restore all to the Union again, from the fact that they did not want union with the Northern States, let them make whatever concessions they would. In fact there were some who appeared to be for making the breach greater in order to draw those States yet content to remain in the Union into the affray, and thus unite all the slave States into a Southern Confederacy. See 11, 12, 13, 14, 15, 16, 17, 18, 19, 20, 21, 22, 23, 24.

Another thing that no doubt tended to inflame the North and cause them to take up arms sooner against the South, was the threats at the South of attacking Washington City, and probably other cities at the North at an early day. See 25, 26, 27, 28, 29.

It seems that we might soon have had peace, and have had an honorable one too, with the exception probably of the Territories, for there was a great reaction taking place at the North in favor of the South. See 30, 31, 32. And further, Rhode Island, Maine and Wisconsin had repealed their Personal Liberty Bills, and Massachusetts had modified hers.

But the main difficulty in the way was, that many of our leading men did not want union, and therefore refused to work for it, the breach in the meantime becoming greater. But if the counsels of the conservative men had prevailed, we should now have had peace instead of war. But the extreme politicians of the North and the South have precipitated the country into dissolution and bloodshed. They have created a future through which no eye can penetrate—a future of blackness, of darkness teeming with armies. In all probability these troubles will eventually result in the downfall of many of these unprincipled politicians North and South.

So after summing up the whole, if the Southern authorities acted at the taking of Fort Sumpter as has been represented, it seems that they did not act for the best to avoid a difficulty. If they could have got possession of the fort after it was evacuated, it seems they ought to have been satisfied without desiring that they should surrender as prisoners of war, when as yet there had been no war.

And if Col. Lamon proposed a vessel of war to bear them off in, I think they should have accepted it, though it had not been fully in accoordance with their wishes. I think they had better have yielded a little than to have stuck out and brought on such direful consequences. Maj. Anderson and his soldiers, in all probability, went to the forts of Charleston in a war vessel, and if the authorities at Washington desired that they should depart in one, I can't see why they could not, consistently with the honor of the State and Confederate States, have been permitted to have done so. I fear that 13, 15 and 17 were in too many hearts of the Southern people to admit of an easy adjustment. It seems they were in for secession, and nothing else, which in my opinion would have been all right if all that wanted to secede had done so by the voice of their people, and had set up their own government and said no more about it. But it seems that there were some persons who were for getting as many as they could in this secession move by peaceable means, and then in order that they might draw the balance of the slave

States, yet content to remain in the Union, into the affray, they must kick up a dust and have a fight at Fort Sumpter, right or wrong, when it appears that it might have been honorably avoided, at least for a time.

I think it would have been better if the Southern authorities had not been so hasty in cutting off the supplies from Fort Sumpter. They might, I think, without any danger to their cause, have permitted Maj. Anderson at least to have got supplies from Charleston. This would have given more time for the settlement of the difficulties.

But they knew that the remaining slave States had generally passed resolutions against coercion. They probably desired the co-operation of these States, thinking that it would present a more formidable front, and thus tend to back out the North and avoid bloodshed. About this time there were a good many persons of other States dabbling in the affairs at Charleston, which did not concern them. These instances have already been given. It is also stated that Maj. Anderson had agreed to give up the fort Monday at 12 o'clock if he was not provisioned in the time.

In conversation with a soldier that assisted at the taking of Fort Sumter, he said that Maj. Anderson had agreed to give up the fort Monday, the 15th, if the United States flag was not fired on in the time; and he said the reason they did not wait until then and get the fort in that way was, that they were afraid the Federal fleet would run in and reinforce them before that time.

There appears to be conflicting statements, and in these times it is hard to get at absolute certainty, but I give the facts as nigh as I can and leave the reader to judge for himself. The following will probably throw some light upon the subject.

The following correspondence was telegraphed from Montgomery, Ala., to Ex President Tyler by his son, who was at that place:

CHARLESTON, April 8th, 1861.

To L. P. Walker, Dear Sir:—An authorized messenger, from Lincoln has just informed Gov. Pickens and myself that provisions will be sent to Fort Sumter, peaceably if they can, forcibly if they must."

G. T. BEAUREGARD.

MONTGOMERY, April 10th, 1861.

"*To General Beauregard, Charleston*:—If you have no doubt of the authorized character of the agent who communicated to you the intention of the Washington Government to supply Fort Sumter by force, you will at once demand its evacuation; and if this be refused, proceed in such a manner as you may determine to reduce it. Answer.

L. P. WALKER.

CHARLESTON, April 10, 1861.

To L. P. Walker:—The demand will be made tomorrow at 12 o'clock.

G. T. BEAUREGARD.

MONTGOMERY, April 10, 1861.

To General Beauregard, Charleston:—Unless there are special reasons connected with your own condition, it is considered proper that you make the demand at an earlier hour. L. P. WALKER.

CHARLESTON, April 10.

To L. P. Walker:—The reasons are special for 12 o'clock. G. T. BEAUREGARD.

CHARLESTON, April 11th, 1861.
To L. P. Walker:—Demand sent at 2 o'clock. Allowed until 6 o'clock to answer.

CHARLESTON, April 11th, 1861.
To L. P. Walker:—Maj. Anderson replied, "I have the honor to acknowledge the receipt of your communication demanding the evacuation of this Fort, and to say in reply thereto, that it is a demand with which I regret that my sense of honor and of my obligations to my Government prevents my compliance." He adds verbally: "I will await the first shot, and if you do not batter us to pieces, we will be starved out in a few days." Answer.

G. T. BEAUREGARD.

MONTGOMERY, April 11th, 1861,
To Gen. Beauregard, Charleston;—We do not desire needlessly to bombard Fort Sumpter. If Maj. Anderson will state the time at which, as indicated by him, he will evacuate, and agree that, in the meantime, he will not use his guns against us, unless ours should be employed against Fort Sumpter, you are authorized thus to avoid the effusion of blood. If this or its equivalent, be refused, reduce the Fort, as your judgment decides to be the most practicable.

L. P. WALKER.

CHARLESTON, April 12th, 1861.
To L. P. Walker:—He would not consent, I will write to day.

G. T. BEAUREGARD.

CHARLESTON, April 12, 1861.
To L. P. Walker:—We opened fire at 4 30 A. M.
G. T. BEAUREGARD.

CHAPTER IV.

FURTHER PARTICULARS.

Althoug the remaining slave states had generally passed resolutions against coercion, the authorities of the Southern Confederacy did not wait to be coerced, but fired the first guns themselves.

On the 3rd of January, 1861, a vessel loaded with ice from Boston and bound to Savannah, and which, owing to stress of weather, had put into Charleston harbor, was fired upon. This I believe was the first shot fired.

I will here remark that this vessel was first hailed, or ordered to haul to, and upon her refusing to do so, she was fired upon.

January 10th, Star of the West, fired into. Would it not have been well for the authorities at Charleston to have been a little more forbearing. If, as has been said, they could have got possession of the fort by waiting until Monday, would it not have been well to have waited until that time, or until they had attempted to bring in a fleet to provision and reinforce the fort. For they had Morris Island, which lay in the only channel leading to the forts, and to Charleston, strongly fortified, so as to resist probably, any fleet that might be brought against them. They thus had things so arranged, that they could in all probability, have perished out the garrison, let the time have been long or short. Would it not then have been better to have got possession of the fort in this way, or at least to have waited until Monday to have seen whether or not it would then have been given up upon conditions already mentioned. Or if the Southern authorities had made out that they did not care for their holding Fort Sumter, so they did not reinforce it, and have permitted them to supply its garrison, or even permitted them to have got what they desired from Charleston, the probability is that they would soon have got tired of the fort and abandoned it.

But by manifesting too great a desire to get possession of the fort, its occupants, and particularly as they were a little hostile, might have thought that it would be doing the Charlestonians too great a favor to yield so easily, and that they must therefore put them to some little trouble to get in possession thereof; such is human nature. Therefore I think a better plan than bringing on the crisis immediately would have been to have permitted them to have held the fort a month or two, in the mean time having it understood that the fort should not be reinforced. Good time would thus have been given for settling the difficulties and all might have eventually wound up peaceably. And should they have eventually seemed like holding on to the fort too long, it might have been captured a month or two hence as well, probably, as when it was done.

But there were certain people at the South, who have already been hit upon, that seemed to think that by having a little collision at Fort Sumter, the Southern States would all be united, a Southern Confederacy be established and things wind up peaceably. Past experience should have taught them better than this. The ball once put to rolling, there is no telling where it will stop. It is like making iron at the rolling mills. They first hammer down one end of the bloom with a tilt hammer, they then put this end to their rolling mill, it takes hold, draws it through, and thus makes a bar of iron. Even so with our difficulties. The fight commenced at Fort Sumter, has drawn the whole nation into the affray, and when or how it is to end, is yet to be told.

I will illustrate this a little farther by giving a story that I have frequently heard an old gentleman relate.

He said upon a certain night he found himself about three miles from home. Where he had been, or what his business was I do not now recollect. As he was going along homeward, he saw a light suddenly appear in the road before him, which went on in the same direction he was going. He could see something like pitch dropping from it, drops that would burn as they fell towards the ground. He thus kept on for some time, the light keeping before him, all the time, but what bothered him was, that he could see no person with the light. It appeared to be going on of itself. At last it went out beside the road and stoped behind a large pine. Up to this time, our friend says he had not experienced any fear, but as he began to approach the pine, he began to get a little kinder scared, and just as he got against the pine, he thought about the thing jumping out and catching him, and the first thing he knew, he found himself running. A start he said was all he wanted. The farther he ran, the worse he got scared. It was as before said, about three miles home, and he ran every step and jumped two or three fences in the time. At length he reached home, almost scared to death, and out of breath, and bolting against the door he took it off of the hinges, and the door and all came down in the middle of the floor. This nearly scared his old Lady to death. But they talked it over and after a while they both, I believe, recovered from their fright.

I have frequently heard this old gentleman relate this story, and from a long acquaintance with him, I can say that I have no reason to dispute his word. It may have been shown him, probably as a warning in some way.

He said after he got started, the farther he ran the worse he got scared, and the less probability, it seems, there was of his taking up. He thus ran his race quite through, and as a last act, demolished his door and scared his old lady as aforesaid.

So with our difficulties. It was much easier to have avoided them before taking a start, than it is now to stop them, after they have commenced. Each day creates greater difficulties, and renders it more difficult to reconcile the two sections.

Wars may be compared to law-suits, and Dr. Johnson compares people at law to two persons dipping their heads under water, and daring each other to hold under the longest. Wars and law-suits are generally not terminated until one or the other of the parties become exhausted of means, and therefore can't carry them any farther.

In the case of our friend, we said that his getting frightened and running, ultimately frightened his old lady; so he was not the only sufferer in consequence of his getting frightened. So with this war that is now upon us. The fight commenced at Fort Sumter has drawn all, both great and small, throughout the entire length and breadth of our land, into these troubles. Even the female sex has been drawn into the affray, and many a bitter tear has been shed by them, though they had nothing to do in bringing on the war. The good and the bad suffer together. Our leading men should by all means, as much as possible, avoid a beginning of such difficulties.

The immediate cause of the Revolutionary war was, I believe, the tax of three pence a pound on tea, and the blockade of the port of Boston. The East India Company had sent large amounts of tea to various American ports; that which was sent to Boston the Bostonians were determined to have nothing to do with; and not only that, but a party disguised as Indians went on board their ships and staved and emptied their cargoes into the sea. The mother country determined to punish the Bostonians for their disobedience, as a father would a disobedient son, and without any thought, I presume, of bringing on a war, had the port of Boston blockaded. In the meantime a little fight had occurred between some of the soldiers and Bostonians, in which there was three of the latter killed. The fight thus commenced soon ripened into the Revolutionary war, which lasted eight years.

The war of 1812 was mainly brought about, I believe, by the impressment of four seamen from off the Chesapeake, Commodore Baron commanding, by Captain Humphries, of the Leopard. Thus we see that great effects frequently spring from little causes.

CHAPTER V.

PRESIDENT LINCOLN ISSUES HIS PROCLAMATION CALLING FOR 75,000 TROOPS.

April 15, 1861, President Lincoln issued his proclamation calling for 75,000 troops. Requisitions were made upon Virginia, North Carolina, Tennessee, Missouri, Kentucky, Arkansas and Maryland, to furnish their quota of these troops. The States mentioned refused to obey the call, and what I think was a great deal worse, they went immediately out of the Union in consequence. I believe in doing thus, these States, at the least, acted hastily. Any one reading the history of our country at that time will, doubtless, admit that there was a need of more soldiers to carry out government purposes. For Washington City had been menaced, and probably other cities North, as has been already shown. He had to have more troops or give up the government, that was certain, for with the troops he already had, he could not have assigned more than 2000 to the most important stations, and what would they have been to the strong armies then being raised in the South.

We will say that if the President had not called on these States mentioned to have furnished their quota of men they would have been angry, and I think more justly too, for he would then evidently have been looking on them with distrust, as much as to say, you are not the men that I want to carry out my government. I want men of my own party who elected me to office, for upon them I can depend.

And after he called on these States to furnish their quota they were still angry, and so what was he to do? Sit still and let the usurpers of power at the South overrun the Capital and tear down the government. I call them usurpers, because they had not derived their power directly from a majority of the constitutional voters of the South as has already been shown. If the question of secession had been submitted to a popular vote of the people for decision, and they had said do thus and so, then, in my opinion, it would all have been right. But the way it was, the politicians, I think, were the men that had the most of the say so in the matter.

Much fault has been found of the President because he called for these troops without waiting for the authority of Congress, or without first convening Congress, the right they say to raise armies and declare war belonging solely to that body. I will here remark that at the time of issuing his proclamation calling for 75,000 troops, that he also ordered the convening of both houses of Congress, to take place on the 4th of July following. This, owing to circumstances was, I presume, as soon as it could well be done; because, before Congress could be convened, there first had to be elections held in seven States, and in all fifty representatives chosen, after leaving out the seceded States. Of these, thirteen would have been chosen in Virginia on the 23d of May, the regular day of her State election. So it seems that he could not have convened Congress and raised the necessary troops in a much shorter time than three or four months, had he waited first to have convened Congres , and in that time it might have been too late.

You will please permit me to state here, that if I am not wrongly informed, the Constitution of the United States, permits the President to call out the Militia in case of an invasion or insurrection against a State or the General Government. And inasmuch as secession was not provided for in the Constitution, I can't see how it is that Lincoln acted unconstitutionally in issuing his proclamation calling for the 75,000 troops. If such a course as was then being taken in the South be not termed an insurrection against the general government I don't know what you would call one.

These last States, Virginia, North Carolina, &c., seceded from the fact that they thought the President wanted these troops, with which to coerce the seceded States. I will here remark that if at the time those first seven States seceded that there was a majority of the constitutional voters in these states in favor of remaining in the Union, that I believe the President to have been right in issuing this Proclamation in order to put down the rebellion, but then, if there was a majority in favor of going out of the Union, then I believe him to have been wrong. But the way it was, we can't tell whether the majority of the constitutional voters in these states were in favor or against secession, and therefore can't tell whether or not Lincoln was right in issuing his proclamation calling for these troops. But if these states seceded by a minority vote, unless the general government had taken steps to coerce or bring them back, there was no other power left to do so, and if let alone the first step towards an Aristocratical Government would thus have been taken. It is therefore to be regretted that all the states that chose to secede had not submitted it to the popular vote of their respective states for ratification or rejection. Our course would then have been more clearly defined. I will here remark that I presume I am as much opposed to Black republican misrule and oppression as any one, but I was not for taking such a decisive step until such treatment had been shown towards us, and if it had thus become necessary for us to act, I think it should have been submitted to the people to give their assent or dissent thereto. We have a brave, bold highminded set of people, and had the North have infringed on their rights, I don't think they would have been long in offering a proper resentment, and if the causes had been justifiable, I not only consider it their privilege but actually their duty to have seceded or withdrawn from the general government. One great reason for arguing that the ordinance of secession should have been submitted to the people is, that whatever would have been right in the matter, I think they would have done ; if it had been right, and justice had demanded it, they would doubtless have seceded, but if the causes had not been justifiable, I don't think they would have seceded, They did not have any ends to accomplish like many of the politicians. They would therefore have considered the matter cooly and deliberately and would not have seceded, I don't think for trivial causes.

Inasmuch as it was mixed up with uncertainty, whether or not the majority ruled at the seceding of the several States, would it not have been well for the governors of the states yet remaining in the Union to have made some inquiries of the President as to what disposition he proposed making of these troops, before seceding and bringing on such direful consequences. Maryland furnished her quota of troops, and the President gave the Governor of that State a pledge that he would use the troops thus furnished only in defense of their own State or Washington City. Perhaps he might have made the same disposition of the troops from this State, had our Governor have complied with his Proclamation, or even showed a disposition to do so. Or he might probably have begged off from furnishing any troops, and yet remained in the Union, and particularly as the Northern States had furnished more than the 75,000. I don't here, wish to be understood as advising that we must stoop to any thing dishonorable in order to remain in the Union.

The first thing I think, for the States to do after seceding, even if they had done so by a popular vote, was to take care of themselves, and to fight when force was brought against them, and not to have threatened an unprovoked attack against Washington City and other points North. The North declare that it was the threat against the North, principally Washington City, that first caused them to take up arms against the South.

CHAPTER VI

LETTERS OF MARQUE ISSUED.

Letters of marque were issued by President Davis on the 17th of April, 1861. This did not appear to be guarding either our homes, or our rights, but was at once, I think, taking the war to where it need not be. This circumstance reminds me of a remark of Benjamin Franklin, upon a certain occasion. He said many times a man having but little money is more free with it than if he had a good deal, in order that people may not think he has but little. So with the Southern Confederacy. They having but few or no vessels, wished to make up for the deficiency by making this vain boast to the world.

Again the Southern authorities passed what is called the sequestration act, confiscating all property or debts due Northern people. Was this justice? Was it right? Perhaps these sums due Northern citizens, may have been for work and labor done, and this was sold here to the people of the South at fair prices and with a perfect understanding that they were to be paid. Perhaps there are persons at the North who have incurred debts in getting up this merchandise ; they there have to pay these debts, but here the property or dues as the case may be, is confiscated and applied to government purposes. Is this Justice? Perhaps these claims, too are going to our friends at the North, men whose hearts are with us. Their claims, too are confiscated. These claims do not belong to government. They never purchased them nor paid value for them; therefore in my opinion, they had no right to interfere therewith. I think, they should have been let alone, and at the close of the war let the people of the south pay to those of the North their just dues and vice versa, Confiscating these dues will, I think, only cause the war to be waged more fiercely against us.

CHAPTER VII.

PERSONAL LIBERTY BILLS.

Again it may be argued that the north acted unconstitutional in passing those Personal Liberty Bills. So they did. There were originally but thirteen states, twelve of which were slave holding, and slavery was guaranteed under the constitution of 1787. But were they an offense justifiable of secession, breaking up the Union and what is a great deal worse, bringing upon us this horrible war? I trow not. These liberty bills had such a very small effect on us here, that we scarcely knew of their existence until these sectional troubles broke out. If they had been an offense justifiable of secession, why did not the border slave states, that suffered most by them, secede first? They lost probably an hundred fugitives to where the more Southern States lost one. Why then were those extreme Southern States, that hardly ever lost a fugitive, the first to secede? And after all, is secession any remedy for the evil?

Will there not, in all probability, half a dozen flee from their masters and seek homes in Northern States to where there did one before, and without the least hope of their ever being recovered, for in case of separation they will not then, I presume, give us the benefit of the fugitive slave law. If the two sections were separated, would not this thing tend soon to involve them in war again. It is true there has sometimes been opposition made to the owners in recovering their fugitive slaves from the north, but probably there were ten, twenty or even fifty given up peaceably to where there was one forcibly taken from his owner, or one that he was prevented by violence from getting. Generally about those that were recovered peaceably there was nothing said, whilst an account of those that were forcibly taken from their masters, or such as they were prevented from getting, was in almost every news paper throughout the land, and particularly at the South.

It is said by the people of the north that the fugitive slave law has times more than once, caused free persons of color to be enslaved. See 33. I expect though, the number thus brought away was but few, whilst many have escaped from the south to the north who have never been recovered.

In the summer of 1855, there were servants that absconded from the city of Norfolk, Va., in one month alone to the value of about $30,000. If they could stand this and not secede, why could not the people of more southern states, who had lost but very few servants if any, by their absconding to the North. And if these liberty bills had been a grievous and universal thing, were there no way to remedy the evil only in secession. Could not the people of the south have imposed heavy taxes on goods of Northern manufacture, and thus have kept back their goods, and also their vessels that brought them. This would soon have built up the necessary manufactories among us and we would not then have needed their goods. If the trade of the North had thus been cut off and their vessels kept at home, there would have been but few of our servants taken there I assure you. Or if we preferred still to trade with the north to a certain extent, we should have built our own vessls with which to have done our trading, and not have had all our freighting done by northern vessels. This would also, to a very great extent, have stopped the running away of our servants and seeking homes in northern states. This course would also have tended much towards building up the south, in making us a manufacturing and commercial people. It would also have vastly strengthened our money market and would have eventually done away with these money panics, that have been occurring at intervals of a few years for a good many years back. Our overtrading to the North and they overtrading to Europe has been two of the main fruitful causes in bringing about those panics.

In illustration of this I will bring forward some facts.

At the time of President Buchanan's inauguration, there were in the United States some 1400 banks with specie in their vaults to the amount of $63,000,000.

We have been trading to Europe, to the West Indies, and to other powers, to such an extent that we actually traded out all our cotton, tobacco, rice, &c., that we exported, and then sent away annually, $30,000,000 in specie besides. For the single item of coffee we have been paying fifteen and a half million dollars annually. This sum or the amount that our imports exceeded our exports ($30,000,000) had to go in gold and silver, and came indirectly from the vaults of the southern banks, Because the people at the north have to pay specie for these goods what they lack of having exports enough to pay with—mostly southern cotton, rice, tobacco, turpentine, &c. Our merchants then go north and buy these goods and give them in exchange our bank notes. The northern merchants or brokers then send back these notes and with them draw the specie from our banks, and we having no place to draw from principally feel the effects of these money panics. So it will be seen that two years thus trading will exhaust our banks of nearly every dollar in their vaults.

These panics would, doubtless, have been more frequent and of a more serious nature had it not been for the large influx of gold from California.

In a little over ten years gold has been brought from California to the amount, I believe, of $479,000,000. During the fifty years previous there was produced in the whole United States, I believe about $20,000,000 worth. This gold was once with us, but owing to our tariff and system of free trade, is now, to a great extent, in Europe or some other foreign power. All these panics, &c., I think might have been prevented, our servants kept at home, and nobody hurt by putting up a high protective tariff, and, to a great extent, prohibiting both Northern and European manufactures. I think we should have a tariff such as would cause our exports to equal, if not exceed our imports. We have the advantage, and why not make use of it to a certain extent. I would not be for passing such a law as this in retaliation for anything that the North may have done, but I actually think such a law necessary for our well being as a people. We should also have had our own vessels to carry on our commerce. The scale would then soon have turned, and instead of sending our specie out of the country, we should been bringing it in both from the North and from Europe; because we have the cotton, tobacco, rice, turpentine, &c., such as the North and Europe cannot well do without. And we had better, in my opinion, have passed such laws even if we had had to have paid some higher here for the same article of home manufacture. In time competition would have gotten up among our manufacturers, and the articles would thus soon have been brought down sufficiently low. Our paper currency would then pay for these goods, and there would be but very seldom, if ever any, run upon our banks. Our banks would then probably have been on the best foundation of any in the world. No more money panics would then ever have been heard of, for we would always have had plenty of gold and silver among us. Would it not, therefore, have been better to have brought the North to their senses by passing laws to this effect, than it was to kick up at small offences, try the doubtful ordinance of secession, and in place of the lesser evils bring on others infinitely greater?

But it may be argued that we had not the power to pass laws relative to the tariff, &c., whilst in the union. But it seems to me with the rights the states had that each state could have passed a law that would have answered about the same purpose as though it had been passed by the general government. At all events, I think the people of the South had as good a right to pass such laws as these, as the North had to pass those personal Liberty bills, and I think by passing such laws that the north would eventually have been brought to see their error, and that they were as much dependant on, and interested in slave labor as the people of the South. They might thus eventually have been brought to see their error and as a consequence repealed those offensive Liberty bills. At all events I think such a course would have kept off these difficulties for a considerable time if it had not effectually healed them I think by taking the proper course that these difficulties might have been settled peacably, but even if they could not, let us have shown the disposition to keep them off as long as possible, so that if the worst did come that the fault of no part of it could be laid to us.

The last hope of bringing about a reconciliation should first have been lost before bringing on such a dreadful calamity as a civil war. Let us hope that the storm may soon blow over, and that these difficulties may soon be settled honorably, fairly, and peacably, and without any farther spilling of blood.

CHAPTER VIII.

TREATMENT OF SERVANTS.

Again it may be argued by the people of the North that in many instances, the people of the South are so cruel to their servants that there was a need of something being passed in the shape of Personal Liberty bills to protect them from harsh treatment.

It is to be regreted that effective laws are generally lacking to protect the poor African from the cruel treatment to which he is sometimes submitted. I am happy to believe, though, that the treatment of servants is fast changing for the better from what it has been. The following rules are intended in the main to apply to the exceptions of good treatment we now and then meeting up with a case, but they are very rare in this section. But still upon these exceptions there should,

I think be some stringent binding laws passed in order to enforce humanity upon them if they will not practice it without. It is no pleasure for me to speak upon this subject as I shall, before I get through the work, but I shall do so solely as as a duty I think I owe to my God and fellow man. Then as before intimated I believe there should be some stringent laws passed restricting the priviliges of cruel masters, for they can and sometimes do, strip and tie their servants and then literally cut their hides to peices with the lash and there is no one to raise his voice in behalf of the poor African. They have also sometimes been paddled with a paddle having holes bored in it, to a horrible degree. He cries and begs for mercy with all his might, but still the cruel lash keeps coming.

There is evidently a law needed in behalf of these people. But the people of the north are not the ones to make it. The people should here, I think, have taken it into their own hands, and have passed laws such as would have insured their general good treatment.

I therefore, think a law somewhat like the following would be well.

That no master, nor other person, should at any one time give his servant more than six stripes upon his bare back, unless it be for some very grievous offense. In that case, if the master should be desirous of giving his servant more than six stripes at any one time, let him take the offending servant before some acting justice of the peace, and there make his complaint against him, and if the magistrate shall so adjudge, he may then and there give his servant as many as thirty-nine lashes upon his bare back.

This plan would, I think, have a good moral effect

upon the servant, because he would be ashamed to be thus publicly whipped, and one such whipping would, I think, do more good in restoring order and discipline that half a dozen would given privately. I therefore think that he would endeavor to the utmost to avoid such a whipping by doing his duty as nearly as possible, from the fear of being thus exposed. Such a course of treatment would have as much or probably more to do in keeping them in their line of duty than the punishment itself. Therefore let us use means as much as lay in our power, to bring them to their duty without resorting to rought means. But let us hope that there would never be any need for going over the six stripes and not even that many, if it can well be avoided.

There should evidently be some restrictions put upon cruel masters, for they frequently inflict greater punishment than they are aware of, as they feel no part of the pain thus inflicted themselves. If a master should violate this law, i. e. give more than six stripes at any one time, only as prescribed above, let the servant thus treated go out free. See 34.

I don't wish to be understood as advocating the doc- that slavery is wrong. If God has placed them in a condition to be slaves, and decreed that they should be such, I don't know that it should particularly concern us more than to treat them well.

Whether or not it be right and consistent with the will of Almighty God to own slaves, I am unable at present to tell. We find them here, and I think the best thing that we can do with them at present, is to keep them and treat them with kindness and humanity and if it be not consistent with the will of Almighty God, to keep them thus, He will doubtless in time make it known to us.

Where servants are properly and well treated they are in all probability, in a much happier and better condition than they would be, freed and at the north, whither many of them have gone, or in their native country, Liberia.

Travelers universally give it as their opinion, (so far as my knowledge goes,) that the servants at the south, where they are well treated, are in a much happier and better condition than the free blacks at the north are in·

That there were servants in old times admits not of doubt. See 35.

Though from the above it seems that the Hebrews only were commanded or permitted to own servants or bondmen. In justification of this. See 36.

If the Hebrews only were commanded or permitted to own servants or bondmen, it is evident that no other nation hath a right to own them under that command.

The Hebrews were the chosen people of God, and had themselves suffered bondage and various afflictions, and the probability is that this privilege was granted them to make up for some of their reverses, or because they were the special and chosen people of God, our right, therefore to retain or own bondmen under this command, will depend on our establishing that we are of Hebrew descent. I leave the reader to satisfy himself on this point. If we can establish that we are of Hebrew descent, then have we a right to hold bondmen under that provision; otherwise we must derive our right to hold them from some other source.

But if we find that we are not of Hebrew descent, how about it then? Why, as we find them here, and as it is admitted that they are better off here in a state of servitude, than they would be in their native country, Liberia, or in the Northern States free, whither many of them have gone, I don't know what better we can do with them than to keep them here as they are, and treat them well.

They are evidently better off here, provided they are well treated, where they have the light of the Gospel, than they would be in a heathen land. Therefore, transporting them here it seems must have been an advantage to them, provided they are well treated.

Seems like it is more than our brethren at the north should reasonably expect that the blacks of Africa should be transported from the desert waste of a tropical country to one far more genial and fertile, and freed solely at our expense. The original stock of slaves here was purchased by our forefathers, either of slavers, or from those Northern States which have since abolished slavery. And if it were right thus to bring them here and free them solely at our expense, they might as wel argue that we had best continue to spend our money for these people in order to get them to a better country. For no philanthropist, I presume, would argue that it would be best to send the slaves that are here back to the desert wastes of Africa, from whence they came. And there is no Scripture nor moral law that I have ever seen that would go to prove that it is our duty thus to transport them from the desert waste of a tropical country, for the sake of getting them to one far more genial and fertile.

This generation did not bring them here, or cause them to be brought. Therefore in my opinion we are not responsible for their being here. So if their being brought here is a godly or an ungodly act I think neither the credit nor the blame, as the case may be, of any part thereof rest with us. We find them here and as a philanthrophic people I think we should not do any hing to worse their condition, which in my opinion-would be done were they freed and sent back to the parching sands of Africa from whence they came. And if it be wrong to have them here in servitude, it would seem to be our duty to send them back from whence they came.

The servants that are here in my opinion are much better off, where they are well treated, than their brethren in Africa and are likewise probably of some advantage to us here as well as to the people of the north and the various European nations. For they are much better adapted for working the cotton, rice and sugar plantations of the south than the white man is. Because they can labor with impunity among various epidemic diseases of the south, where the white man would soon sicken and die.

I will give an example of this.

During the prevalence of that dreadful scourge, Yellow Fever, in Norfolk in the summer of 1855, there died, I believe, about 3,000 people. During this most distressing time of sickness, suffering and death, the negroes escaped with almost perfect impunity. I only heard of one or two being sick of yellow fever and they might possibly have been sick of some other disease. I can't say with certainty that it proved fatal among the blacks in the first instance, whilst among the whites at the time of its greatest rage, there died nearly one hundred per day. I was there for a considerable time, myself among the fever, and I know that I heard it remarked, that the fever took but little or no effect on the black population. This goes to prove that they are much less liable to be affected by the diseases of warm climates than the whites, and are, therefore much better adapted for working in the cotton, rice and sugar plantations of the South.

But I don't consider this even a justifiable excuse for reducing them to bondage, provided we know or believe it not to be in accordance with God's will, thus to keep them. We not knowing the will of God, with certainty upon this subject, I think we had better keep them as they are for the present, and if it be not consistent with His will to keep them thus, He will, I think, doubtless in time make it known to us, as has been before stated.

Those persons that are so desirous of seeing the servants at the south emancipated, I think would do well to look into the thing and see whether their condition would be bettered by thus freeing them. We have abundant evidence to prove that their condition, as it now is, is generally speaking, a great deal better than that of their free brethren either north or south. Indeed, where they are well treated, they may be said to be among the happiest people in the world. For they generally couple off at an age as early as they are susceptible of. There are no questions of property nor of a worldly character to decide with them, for their women are all like Lycurgus would have those of Sparta, all equal as to property, 37. There are but few or no cases of celibacy among them, and they have but few or no cares as to their rising families; all goes well and in old age, they are taken good care of. So I think, when they are well treated, that they are about the happiest people that the sun shines on.

In order that the reader may know the condition of some countries where emancipation has taken place, I refer him to 38.

CHAPTER IX.

TREATMENT OF SERVATNS—continued.

We will now look at what we call good treatment of servants. That there must be some mode of punishishment for the disobedient, can't be denied by persons knowing anything of the management of servants.

The mode and the degree are the things to be attained to.

When chastising is resorted to, it should be done with a light hand, so as not to cut the skin, and with an eye single to their behefit, giving no more than may be absolutely necessary to insure obedience. Do not mark them up and send them down to their graves bearing the marks of the cruel lash. Some cruel persons in chastising become excited, and the poor negro hollowing and beging for mercy, only excites them and causes them to apply the lash more cruelly. Such persons ought to have a wooden negro to whip upon, that could hollow and beg without the operator knowing but what it was a genuine negro that he was at work upon. It is too much for human flesh to bear such immense torture. Vengeance belongeth to the Lord, and I don't think any one here is authorized to inflict hell upon earth. The Lord will, I think, doubtless hold all such responsible at the last day. Let us govern as much as possible by love and mild means. A servant that is actuated to duty through love and veneration to his master, does his work much more cheerfully, and I may say better too, than one that is driven through fear. Good masters make good servants. Give them good comfortable clothing to wear and of the same kind of food that you partake of yourself. 35.

I think I can sum up in a few words all that is necessary for the good government of servants. Fed well, clothe well, and when it be necessary and unavoidable whip well. You must keep them in subjection either with the rod, or by creating feelings of love and veneration in them towards you as a master.

If you can govern by this latter mode, which is by far the best, there will then be but little or no need of resorting to rougher means. You must though keep order and discipline among them or they will soon render you so as not to be able to treat them well, for left to their own will they soon cease to work to much advantage. They would soon get to be like bees when transported to the island of Jamaica. They then soon cease to lay up honey and divert themselves by flying about the sugar mills and stinging the hands at work. The reason that they thus cease to lay up honey I presume is that they can always get plenty of the necessary food without that trouble. Past experience has generally proven this to be the case with servants where they have either been emancipated or left to their own will even. In either case they soon get to be like the bees—cease to work to much advantage.

But as has already been remarked, good masters make good servants. Try as much as possible to get them to take an interest in affairs as though they were their own. And in order that your servants may thus become interested in your affairs, I think it necessary for you to give your business your personal attention and become interested in it yourself before you can except your servants to take a proper interest in your affairs.

Give them time to work for themselves, half of each Saturday we will say, to make something to buy necessaries with. This course will cause time fly as it were and they will be apt to attend more cheerfully to their business during the week with the hope in the end of working some for themselves.

I will here mention somewhat a novel plan for the treatment of disobedient servants. There is a gentleman not a great ways from this place who, for disobedience of his servants, causes a table to be spread with the choicest dainties he has; the offender must then sit down and take a hearty repast. This is all the punishment he inflicts, very rarely if ever resorting to any rougher mode. I think they are under as good discipline, attend to business as closely, and are likewise as proffitable to their owner as any in the whole country. The feeling of love here predominates. It has a moral effect on them, and causes them to take care of things as though they were their own. Let us hope that laws will soon be passed concerning these people, such as at least will clear us from having any sin to answer for on their account.

CHAPTER X.

THE BLOCKADE ESTABLISHED.

Arms having been appealed to, President Lincoln, on the 19th April, 1861, issued his proclamation ordering the ports of the seceded States to be blockaded. Eight days thereafter, or on the 27th, he issued another proclamation ordering the still farther blockade of the ports of Virginia and North Carolina, the inhabitants thereof having seized upon certain of their forts, &c., and Virginia had also seceded on the 17th of April. North Carolina did not secede until the 20th of May. Tennessee, Arkansas, and I believe, Missouri, soon seceded also.

June the 10th, the battle of Great Bethel near Yorktown, Va., was fought. The war thus commenced soon became general. The history of it from that time down to the present I leave with the reader.

Let us now go back and take another view of the beginning of these difficulties.

I will ask the question, was secession under the circumstances best? I will give it as my opinion that the causes were not justifiable, and that it was therefore not for the best. The last hope of bringing about a reconciliation should, I think, first have been lost before taking such a step. It is easy to tear up a government but hard to put one right again.

About the time secession was taking a good start among us, I heard several gentlemen in their speeches assert " That it is now no time to talk but a time to act, the time for talking, they said, had passed." And farther after the war had commenced, it was a common thing for this same class of men to say, "That it is now no time to talk of the causes of the war, how it came about," &c. The war, they said is upon us and we must fight out. Right or wrong, it seems we must fight out without once looking back to see whether or not we are right. If we be wrong how can we expect heaven to crown our efforts. I at the time differed in opinion with these gentlemen, and I do not believe that it is yet too late to talk. In fact I believe it is a time that our greatest and most conservative men should be called forth, so as, if possible, to settle this distressing question without any farther shedding of blood.

The first thing then that I think we should do, even now at this late hour, is to go back and look into the causes of this war; with an impartial eye, and if we find that we are in an error, or that the fault of any part of it rests with us, let us set in right there to work, and not cease until we change it to what is right By doing this is the only way that we may expect to get upon a sure foundation. If in an error, I think we had better to retract than to continue in it, for the Scriptures, I think, somewhere say that "The Lord will abhor the deceitful and bloody man." Then until we first conform to His will as near as we can as a nation and people, how can we expect Him to give us success in spilling the blood of our fellow man. Then let us inspect this fabric that has been rearing since secession took its start closely, and if we find any thing in the structure that is wrong, let us tear down and build of anew whatever the cost. If we can detect any error in this fabric, I think we had better do this than for it to eventually tumble and fall and crush us in the ruins.

And if there be manifest error in it, until this be done I look upon the prayers ascending from our pulpits for the success of our arms, right or wrong as it were, as solemn mockery. I think it unbecoming a minister of the gospel, either North or South, to pray that we may succeed by force of arms; that we may kill, oh, a great many thousand of the enemy, and drive them back ut terly discomfited and sorely by the force of arms!

In order that I may make my position plainer, I will use the following illustration: We will say that a master workman gives an apprentice a job of work to do, and he, instead of doing the work well, bungles over it in some way, or perhaps does a part of it wrong. He then applies to his master for more work. Does he give it to him? No! He tells him to go and do the work well that he gave him before, and he will then give him more.

So of our sectional truobles. If we can find anything in the past relative to our government, or to these sectional troubles that is wrong, right back there we should go and begin, and not cease until it is done right.

I will illustrate this a little farther: We will say that one professes religion; gets a fresh and bright hope. For awhile all goes well, but after awhile temptations arise; he is seduced and led away from duty; he sins against heaven and Divine light. The Scriptures somewhere say to the effect that "If any after having received Divine light, fall away, it is impossible to renew them again unto repentance, seeing they crucify Christ afresh, and put him to an open shame." What then! They can't be saved in their sins, and they can't repent and get religion over again, and give in another christian experience, for that would be crucifying Christ afresh. What then must they do? Why all such doubtless recollect the first sin, and even the first time they committed this sin after professing, and right back to that place they must go and get forgiveness for this sin, before they may expect to make much progress in grace. Were it not for the words "unto repentance," in the text, it would certainly be a bad case with all that backslide; and, though they can't profess religion and get it over again, they can go back and seek forgiveness for what they have done, and if they seek in the right way, they will be apt soon to obtain it, and be led forth in the green pastures in which they once roamed, and things thus all be brought right again. But as I said before, until they do this, they need not expect to make much progress in grace.

So as regards our country. Somebody is wrong. Somebohy is in fault and responsible for the much blood being spilt, the many valuable lives lost, the much suffering produced, and for the many orphans and widows made by this great and mighty struggle. And that fault wherever it is, or whatever persons may be in it, is doubtless based in wickedness.

I therefore think that a better prayer for our ministers would be to pray, that those that are in fault and principally instrumental in bringing on these difficulties may be brought to see their error, that their course may be changed, and that they may soon unite for settling these difficulties peaceably, honorably and fairly, and without the farther spilling of blood.

Notwithstanding the doubtfulness of the justness of some of our proceedings, our clergy and laity still implore the God of heaven for aid and protection, and that they may be successful in this their undertaking, and expect Him to bend as it were to suit their cases, and to aid them, when the justice of their appeal to arms is at least questionable. If the foundation of the structure be wrong, you may build upon it until the fabric shall reach the skies and the whole fix is wrong. The first thing, I think, that should be done in. that case is to tear down and begin of anew. Lay the foundation right, then build upon it in the same way, and we may then expect to have a permanent government.

I am not like a certain Ex-Governor in an adjoining state, and who is now a general in the Confederate army, who in a speech upon a certain occasion said, " My motto is my country; may it always be right; but right or wrong my country." I look upon such as this as misguided patriotism. I think all true patriots should be for their country when right, and if· their country be wrong, let them use their utmost endeavors to put it right, and if they fail to do this, then let them go for what is right. For if one's country is wrong, what better evidence need we to want that our government is administered by bad wicked men; I therefore, think, instead of backing them, endorsing their proceedings, and imploring God's protection for same, that a better plan would be to strike a blow, where in my opinion, it rightly belongs. Strike it at those bad wicked men in power. Remove them from office, and instead thereof, put in good pious men, men who hold direct communion with God. You may then expect soon to have a good and permanent government, for such men will not go for any thing wrong if they know it.

I will illustrate this idea a little.

There was some years ago upon one of our western rivers, a steamboat making one of her regular trips.

Among the passengers was one who had about his person a large sum of money. Night coming on, he had requested of the Captain a private room, which was given him, and he had retired. From some cause or other, probably from the boat becoming more crowded, it became necessary for him to have a comrade, accordingly there was one put in with him. Our friend says that in the very looks of his guest, he thought he could detect the robber, and his very long beard gave him a still more savage appearance; so he eyed him closely. But this gentleman, after undressing himself knelt down and prayed a short fervent prayer. He prayed for the welfare of his wife and little ones at home, for a safe trip, &c. He then got up and got in bed. Our friend after seeing this, had no fears of his companion. He soon dropped off to sleep, awoke in the morning and all was right.

This is the effect of true religion. Government in the hands of such men, all will be well. The prayers of such people avail much. For they will not pray nor go for any thing that they do not believe to be in accordance with the will of Almighty God.

If we could put through any design which we do not believe to be in accordance with the will of Almighty God, we should not do it, though it might at present appear to be of much advantage to us. We may rest assured, that sooner or later the judgment of God will be upon us; for any thing built not in accordance with His will can't stand.

I will mention for instance the case of Moses at Kadesh in the desert of Zin. The Isralites there became thirsty for water and chode with Moses for bringing them up out of Egypt. Moses was there commanded to speak to the rock before their eyes, and it should give forth his water. "Take the rod, and gather thou the assembly together, thou and Aaron thy brother, and speak ye unto the rock before their eyes; and it shall give forth his water, and thou shalt bring forth to them water out of the rock; So thou shalt give the congregation and his beasts drink." Numb. 26: 8.

Moses smote the rock with his rod twice, the water flowed abundantly for the people and beasts. All drank and it appeared that all might be well, but not so; Moses had not obeyed the command of the Lord. he had smiten the rock instead of speaking to it; and for violating this command, he was prohibited from entering the Land of Promise. Though the smiting of of the rock had probably caused the water to flow as it would have done had he spoken to it, yet he had not obeyed the command of God. Though he had by command smitten the rock at Horeb and caused the water to flow there, I presume pretty much at it did here, and though he had smiten it probably unthoughtedly, thinking that he must now bring the water in the same way that he did at Horeb, and particularly as he was commanded to take his rod with him, yet it would not all excuse him, and for disobeying this command he was permitted only to behold the Promised Land. Therefore to obey a command of God we must do just what is commanded, nothing more nor less. Though it may appear to go well at the time, as it did with Moses, yet there will be apt sooner or later to be a curse of some kind upon the offender.

What I wish to prove by the foregoing is that as wars can't be established in justice according to the word of God, a curse of some kind certainly awaits the guilty party, though at present they may even be victors.

Wisdom is better than weapons of war; but one sinner destroyeth much good.

Let us first be sure we are right then may we reasonably expect God's aid in crushing out our enemies.

I will here state again that I do not believe the causes were justifiable for secession for the following reasons and that therefore, at least, a portion of the wrong must be on our side.

The President was constitutionally elected, though by a party antagonistic to the interests of the South (mostly as regards the teritories) had their principles been caried out. Notwithstanding this I think we should have waited until he had done some unconstitutional act before seceding and bringing on such direful consequences. Because though of the Republican party he had in his inaugural, I believe, stated that he had no desire or disposition to interfere with the institutions of the South, meaning slavery.

And in some of his speeches he said I always told you that we would beat you ; that could have been kept off longer by nominating Stephen A. Douglas for the Presidency than in any other way, but now that we have beaten you I expect you wish to know what we are going to do with you. I will tell you what we will do with you. It is my desire to treat you as near like Washington and Jefferson and Madison did as I can.

He said upon another occasion that there should be no blood spilt during his administration if he could help it.

Again, to the division in the democratic ranks, and as a consequence, running two democratic canidates instead of one, is mainly attributable the cause of Mr. Lincoln's election. Had they have remained united the Republican party in all probability could not have come into power for many years to come, even if it ever had. It then appears bad that the Democratic party must split up and make a breach through which the Republican party came into power, and then, merely because they came in after the way was opened for them, they must disrupt every tie and go immediately out of the union.

Had the Republican party been largely in the majority so as to be able to carry through any design they wished and had also have threatened speedily to have taken our rights from us we could not have done any more than we did. We could not have taken a more decided stand against them than we did, even if they had threatened to have taken our liberties from us and to deprive us of every thing else that was near and dear to us. But instead of being in the majority we find them largely in the minority as has already been shown. So had we have brought our powers rightly to bear on them as we might have done, we might have kept the ascendancy in spite of them. the people of the Northern States were also to a great extent conservative as I will show before I get through. Under these circumstances I think we should not have acted with so much haste, and particularly as Lincoln's election was owing mainly to the breach in the Democratic party.

The Democratic party split up and made this breach through which the Republican party came into power, but whether or not they did this designedly I am not able to say.

Secretary Floyd had I believe during the Summer of 1860 sent 135.000 stand of small arms, besides large amounts of munitions of war, to the southern forts and arsenals. There was then no talk nor thought itself among the people of these coming difficulties. When these states seceded they seized upon these arms, which made them able to offer a much greater resistance in the struggle when it did come.

Did these states secede because they thought the President would do them an injury? He was evidently powerless to do this even had he been desirious of so doing. In the first place he had rendered himself harmless by his own words. He would first have had to have eaten them before he could have offered or done any harm to the Southern people.

And more than than this, there was a majority in both branches ot Congress against him. In the House of Representatives there was a majority of thirty against him, and in the Senate there was a majority of from four to eight against him. With this majority against him the Senate could have appointed him a cabinet of the opposite party, had they have chosen to exercise their power, and he would have been compelled to have acted with a cabinet opposed to his views as did

George the III (a tory) king of England who was compelled to act with a whig cabinet, who had to ask the whigs to appoint his ministers and who had to receive a cabinet utterly opposed to his views.

Again, there was not only a large majority of the popular vote against Lincoln as President, but upon top of this there was a large gain against his party at the next state elections. In the present Congress (at the time of Lincoln's election,) the States of Rhode Island and Conneticut had six Republican members in Congress. In the next they have four Democrats and but two Republicans. The State of New York had in the present Congress twelve Republican members. In the next she has but four. There was likewise large gains in most if not all of the other Northen States. Even Springfield Illenois the place of Mr. Lincoln's residence, and which gave him a handsome majority at the Presidential election, had turned over to be democratic. There had also gone up a petition to Congres, from the City of New York, I believe, with 37,754 assigners, praying the settlement of the question by adopting the Crittendon plan. The list was 1,168 feet long. There was also the New York State Convention that wished the question settled by adopting the Crittendon plan, which would have averted civil war and restored peace to the country. They wanted this left to the people—a fair way of settling. If this could only have been done, I think we would soon have had peace. All these things taken together, I think goes to prove conclusively that the people at the north to a great extent were conservative and also willing to yield. If the politicians could have been got out of the way, I don't think the people would have had any difficulty in settling the troubles and restoring quietude to the country, if it had been submitted to them at the *ballot box* after the following plan. Let the people of the slave states first have voted, all the states voting together, whether or not they were willing to have a law passed for the better treatment of servants, something like what has already been mentioned, I think this would have passed by a large majority, for could any christian humane man have done any thing else than have gone for it. We will say then this passed. The northern people would then have had no excuse for keeping up those personal liberty bills.

Then let the people of the Northern States have voted whether or not they were willing to repeal those personal liberty bills, all the Northern States voting. If a majority of the people had been in favor of repealing them, let them have been repealed in all the states where they then existed, but if there had been a majority in favor of these bills, I think they should have been placed on the Statute Books of all the Northern States—let them have gone the whole hog or none. If they had thus voted, in favor of these personal liberty bills, after we had carried ours as aforesaid, I think there would have been but one thing left for us to do—that would have been to secede. But if it had thus been necessary for us to secede, I think we should have done so according to Ex-President Filmore's plan. "Let the states have called a general convention, and let them have seceded peaceably." There was no need of having fighting about it. But I think if the Northern States had voted in favor of these personal liberty bills, that a Convention of the Southern States would have been all that was necessary. Then if they had passed the ordinance of secession, I think it should have been submitted to the popular vote of the Southern States for ratification or rejection. If a majority of the people had thus wanted to have gone out of the Union, I don't think there is any Prince upon earth that should have had power to coerce or keep them in the Union, and vice versa.

But if those personal liberty bills had been submitted to a popular vote of the people at the north, I fully believe that nineteen out of twenty would have voted for their repeal.

I will here remark that the people of the Southern States should first have voted, because if the mistreatment of servants be an offense, it is of longer standing than those personal liberty bills, and should therefore have been removed first.

A law passed for the better treatment of servants and one for the repeal of those personal liberty bills, would, I think have been two very important steps towards bringing about a reconciliation between the two sections. In fact these two things done, I don't see anything in the way at all to have kept from a speedy and peaceable adjustment.

These troubles might in my opinion have been settled by our Congress, both the National and Peace, had we have had the right men in these places, but in my opinion we did not have them there. There were too many of them, in my opinion, Ex-Governors, Ex-Presidents and other large officials—men who were too stout in their natures and dispositions to yield any thing. The longer a man remains in public life, the more, I think does he become settled in his opinions, and the less apt he is to yield any thing to the opinions of others. You will please pardon me for saying here, that I do not think any man should hold an office of proffit and honor longer than four years. The people, I think should be the masters and the officers their servants. But the longer these officers stay in power, the more, I think do they come to the conclusion that they are the masters and the people their servants, and get to be like Hammons, who in the Nashville Convention exclaimed, "the people are to do whatever we command them." I think the reverse of this should be all the time—let the people be the masters and the officers their servants.

It is said that the bark of young trees is better for medical purposes than that of old, and so I think of government officers, I don't though wish to be understood as arguing that young men, before they reach the proper age of experience, make better officers than those older and more experienced—quite the reverse. But I am not for keeping them in office until they grow old in it as it were, and get to believe that the office and people too belong to them. It is true we will find some exceptions to this rule—a few who would make good lifetime officers, but where we find one such a case, I think we will find ninety and nine liable to be led off in the way described.-

Another reason for such a course is, that in many of these offices there is not only good pay but good schooling also. As a member of the Legislature or a member of Congress a man can probably gather practical knowledge as fast if not faster than he can in almost any other way. Therefore in a republican government, I think the thing should be divided as much as possible. In order that I may not be misunderstood, I will here remark that the plan mentioned does not propose that a person shall hold public office only four years during his life. It is only meant that he should not hold any one office but four years. Having digressed from the subject, I will now return to it again.

I will here mention again that Lincoln was evidently powerless to do us any harm, even had he been desirous, for the following reasons. In the first place he had rendered himself powerless by his own words. He would first have had to have eaten them before he could have offered us any harm as before stated.

In the second place, there was a majority against him in both branches of Congress; so he could not have done us any harm, even had he been desirous of so doing.

And in the third place, the party that elected him to power was fast deserting him and joining the Democratic party. So there was no probability of one of his party being elected to the Presidency soon again, if ever.

Why then so hasty to secede? Why not have waited and tried the man until he had at least done some unconstitutional act? Then would have been time enough to have acted.

The truth of it is, we enjoyed a surfeit of Liberty and did not know its priceless value until we had experienced some reverses.

A man in health is not apt to appreciate it fully until he comes to a bed of affliction. He can then look back and see what a great blessing health is. So our people do not or have not in my opinion fully appreciated a good government until they had torn it up and experienced some of the reverses of a civil war.

The Southern States being so hasty to secede and particularly South Carolina puts me in mind of a story that I have frequently heard an old gentleman relate which he says took place in his young days. For the benefit of my readers, I will give this story entire, and in his own language as near as I can. So here goes:

Once upon a time, says he, there came a young man from the adjoining neighborhood and put up for the night. It was Saturday night I believe. This young man was about seventeen or eighteen years old—an age at which inexperienced youths generally think they know more than any one else. There were several young men in the family, some older and some younger than this young man: I having now forgotten his name will denominate it Charley Foolhardy. That night the conversation turned on swimming. Charley expressed great fondness for the exercise, and he could just beat any body out. He talked of it incessantly, and when he went to bed he was still talking about it. Before laying down there was an agreement made between the boys to go a swmming next morning. Next morning good and soon Charley was up and wanted to be off to the river to take the delightful swimming which had been so much on his mind. Persuading to remain until after breakfast, had no effect. So at last nothing else doing he in company with the balance of the young men put off for the river, which was about a quarter of a mile distant. Charley was so anxious to to get into the water that he could not wait until he got to the river to divest himself of his clothing, but commenced pulling off as he went. He pulled off his coat and laid it down here; a little farther he laid down his vest; a little farther still his pants and so on. Before he had got to the river he was stripped off ready, and so taking a running start he pitched into the water as far as he could—over his head the first pass. Instead of being an expert swimmer it was soon discovered that he could not swim any at all, and being in the act of drowning, his comrades—scarcely having time to pull off their shoes, had to jump in with their clothes all on to rescue Charley from a watery grave. Though pretty badly strangled, he was soon restored as good as ever, and had also learned a practical lesson that he could not probably have learned so well in any other way— that he could not swim as easily as he imagined. And so I presume he came to the conclusion that henceforth he would not venture again into deep and unknown waters until he had first learnt how, and knew that he could swim, but would remain on his natural element, land, where he could travel with safety.

I wish to apply the above to the state or states that first seceded. In fact it may now be applied to all the states that have seceded first and last, but most particularly to South Carolina. She appeared to think that secession was all that was lacking and not only refused to wait and act in concert with the ballance of the Southern States, but actually rejected the counsel and advice of some of her older and more experienced sisters, and pitched right into secession whether or not. I think those that were so anxious for secession, after trying it over twelve months, have doubtless come to the conclusion that they can't do much more with it than Charley could at swimming, and that they need help to extricate themselves from their present difficulties as badly as did Charley. It is evident that had not other states have pitched in, that South Carolina would have been drowned ere this, and particularly if this element had have raged with the same fury that it has since done. But by the balance pitching in they have been enabled with much a do, to keep their heads above water. Whether they will eventually drown or arise and come forth from this new element remains yet to be told. I will have occasion to refer again to this similitude before I get through the book, but will prop it for the present.

CHAPTER XI.

OUR GOVERNMENT AS COMPARED WITH OTHERS.

Our government, though defective was probably the best on the face of the globe. Our people seemed to have been unconscious of this. The truth of it is we enjoyed a surfeit of Liberty, and did not know its priceless value until we had torn up our government and experienced some of the reverses of a civil war, as before stated.

A man in health is not apt to appreciate it fully, but let him come to a bed of affliction, he can then look back and see what a great blessing health is. So our people do not or have not in my opinion, fully appreciated a good government until they had torn it up and brought an untold amount of trouble upon themselves.

A good government may be compared to the atmosphere around us, which we breathe. Its benefits are so silent and unseen, that they are seldom thought of or appreciated. We seldom think of the single element of oxygen in the air we breathe, and yet let this simple and unfelt agent be withdrawn, this life giving element be taken away from this all pervading fluid, and what instant and appalling effects would instantly take place throughout all organic creation.

As before remarked, one in health is not apt fully to appreciate it. And a very singular thing is, that one is not apt to do anything to destroy health or body only when in health. I presume you never knew nor heard of any one committing suicide only when in perfect health. It would seem that one under heavy afflictions, such as a painful cancer, would be more apt to commit suicide—but it is to the reverse.

"So much so that in latter stages,
When pains grow sharp and sicknes rages,
The greatest love of life appears."

Even so with our country. Had we have been engaged in a war with some foreign power, or have been in some other difficulty, so as to have had our energies taxed to the utmost to have kept along, the causes that led to secession, and from that to this war, I don't suppose would have been noticed, or thought of itself as being anything serious.

The spelling book, I think somewhere says to the effect, "that the mind unimployed seeks for diversions." We must then, it seems, have kicked up a big dust out of quite a trivial matter, merely for lack of other, and I may say better employment. I therefore look upon it that our government in the midst of her onward march to national honor, prosperity and greatness has committed a national suicide. It is true the old gentleman, uncle Sam, is not yet quite dead, but he is terribly cut up, and will bear the scars of his wounds for many a day, even should he be so fortunate as to get over it. Whether or not the old gentleman will recover, we now can't tell. The disease though is a fearful one. Several great and distinguished personages (Greece, Rome, &c.) have before died of the same disease, and strange to say the very same remedies that killed off those distinguished personages are now being busily applied to the old gentleman with the expectation of healing him, and in the face of all this he is growing a little worse every day. Let us hope that his case will soon be carefully studied, and the proper antiphlogistic remedies (opposed to preternatural heat,) be applied before it be everlastingly too late.

The causes for which we seceded were I think mostly imaginary. Our government like new cider was fast working off its impurities as has already been shown. Things in all probability would soon have wound up peacably had the Southern states remained in the Union a little while until the storm had blown over.

In 1850, South Carolina was desirous of seceding and going immediately out of the Union as has already been stated. Since that time the united States have grown in wealth and power without a paralell I presume in history, even from the creation of the world down to the present time. The material wealth of many of the states have been nearly or quite doubled in that time.

The United States with a mild climate, fertile soil and an abundance of territory were destined it seemed but for these sectional troubles, soon to have taken the front rank among the nations of the globe. Already we were the second in a naval point of view. England was first having I believe over 29,000 vessels. We were next and I believe had over 21,000.

Is there any evidence that had all the Southern states have seceded at that time (1850) that we should thus have grown in wealth, power and greatness? We might and we might not. It is at the least problematical. Let us not throw away a certainty for an uncertainty. A bird in the hand is worth two in the bush. This rapid growth in wealth, power and greatness was doubtless owing to our institutions and system of free government under which we lived, and when we break them up we don't know where the thing will end. We may get it better or we may get it worse, we can't tell.

Some may perhaps argue that we are all that we are, or were rather at the beginning of these sectional troubles, in spite of the general government. But I think it far more probable, considering our short existence as a nation, that we would never have attained to that unrivaleed degree of National honor, presperity and greatnss, and from which we are now so fast waning, but for our civil moral and religious institutions.

It is true, there is perhaps no equal part of the earth with natural recources superior to ours. But how many ages and centuries passed before these capacities were developed to reach this advanced stage of civilization. These same hills rich in ore, same rivers glittering with golden sands, these same valleys and plains, that for fertility and beauty, would have compared favorably with the most beautiful of oriental splendor, were as they had been ever since they came from the hand of the Creator. Uneducated and uncivilized man had roamed over them for how long no history informs us. It was only under our institutions that they could be developed. Their development is the result of the enterprise and indomitable energy of our people, under the operation of the government and institutions under which we have lived. Our people without these, in my opinion, could never have done it. The organization or institutions of a people have much to do with the development of the natural resources of any land or any country. The institutions of a country political, moral and religious, are the matrix in which the germ of their organic stricture quickens into life, takes root and develops in form, nature and character. Our institutions constitute the basis, the matrix from which have sprung all our characteristics of development and greatness.

But destroy our institutions and we thus take the first step towards degredation and ruin. Yea we would fall probably never to rise again.

To show the comparative growth of the United States, I will select here for a parallel the Spanish American Republics.

Population of the United States in 1809 was 6,000,000
" " " 1859, 30,000,000
Spanish American Republics, in 1809, 16,000,000
" " " 1859, 19,000,000
Value of exports from the U. S. 1809, $52,000,000
" " " " 1859, $300,000,000
Spanish American republics 1859, $85,000,000

To prove the condition of these countries and to find out what has always kept them at this low ebb, let us cite an impartial witness.

A writer in the North British Review, speaking of Uruguay, says:

The pastoral resources are very great, but civil war and misrule have seriously retarded their development.

Of Chili, he says: its prosperity would go on advancing were all the obstacles to emigration removed, and the internal peace of the country thoroughly established.

And of the Argentine Confederation, he says:

It is painful to see how so magnificent a country has been misgoverned. Either embroiled with neighboring Republics, or disturbed by intestine feuds, this vast country has scarcely begun to develop her resources. By the foregoing we see that much of the prosperity of a country depends on its government and its institututions. The natural resources of these countries are probably as great if not greater than ours, but owing to bad government and misrule, the vast resources of these countries have never been developed and probably never will be, unless there be a change in government.

We can probably learn a lesson from some of the countries of Europe. Let us see.

We will first look at Greece. There is the same fertile soil, the same blue sky, the same inlets and harbors, the same Ægean, the same Olympus; there is the same land where Homer sung, where Pericles spoke; it is in natnre the same old Greece, but it is living Greece no more. Descendants of the same people inhabit the land, yet what is the reason of this mighty difference. In the midst of present degredation we see the glorious fragments of ancient works of art. Temples with ornamments and inscriptions that excite wonder and admiration, the remains of a once high order of civilization that has outlived the language they spoke. Upon them all Ichabod is writen. Their glory has departed. This is but the fruits of their forms of government. Why is this so? I answer their institutions have been destroyed. They were the matrix from which their grand development sprung, and subsequently nourished them into opulence and power. But when they were destroyed, see how soon their once happy country fell into irrevocable misery and ruin. And if our institutions here be destroyed, there is in all probability no Herculean power that can bring back the life giving spark to kindle them into existence again any more than in that ancient land of eloquence, poetry and song.

The same may be said of Italy.

Where is Rome, once the mistress of the world? There are the same seven hills now, the same soil, the same natural resources, but what a ruin of human greatness meets the eye of the traveller throughout the length and breadth of that most down trodden land. Why have not the people of that heaven-favored clime the spirit that animated their fathers? Why this sad change? I answer, it is the destruction of her institutions that has caused it.

And now my countrymen, we are about pulling down and destroying those institutions under which we have grown so great, and which the patriotic band of of our fathers labored so long and so hard to build up, and which have done so much for us and for the world.

And should this war and sectional troubles continue any length of time, and a complete overthrow of our institutions take place, who is it that can venture the prediction that similar results will not follow here that there did in those deluded ill fated countries. I hope the spirit is yet among our people that will enable us to avert such a direful calamity.

CHAPTER XII.

FURTHER COMPARISON

Our great prosperity in a national point of view was doubtless owing to our institutions and system of free government. And as we were making those rapid strides, destined soon it seems, but for these sectional troubles, to have taken the front rank among the nations of the globe, how much faster did we want to go?

It is true our government though good, had some defects in it. It was with these defects probably the best government on the globe. Nothing of human origin is perfect. But should we not have stuck the closer to our country in her trials, and have labored to have remedied these defects, and not because a man, whom some of us did not like, was elected to the Presidency, have deserted the government and left all in the hands of the Northern people? I think we should. We have as good a right, I think to the government as the North has, and I think instead of abandoning it and leaving all in their hands that it was the time for us to have stuck the closer to the government. Lincoln had sworn to preserve, protect and defend the constitution and if he had have failed to have done so, it was, I think, our duty to have exercised our constitutional power over him and have compelled him to have done so.

The United States before secession were esteemed and respected abroad, and a vessel or an individual had but to hail from the United States to have the highest respect and honor shown them. But how is it now? We are doubtless looked upon by the European Nations with shame and disgust for this disgraceful war that we are now in. Brother against Brother, Father against Son, and Son against Father I may say. Such a war would be a disgrace to a savage nation, let alone to a people claiming in the highest degree to be enlightened.

Our march was onward and upward and, but for these sectional troubles, we bid fair soon to have taken the front rank among the nations of the globe, as before stated. We had an abundance of territory of unsurpassed fertility, a mild, salubrious climate and every facility for making us a great, happy and prosperous nation.

The whole area of the United States
embraced 2,936,166 sq. m'ls.
Of this there were in the free states 612,957 "
" " " " " " slave " 851,508 "
" " " " " " territories, 1,472,061 "

This immense tract of country is more than twenty-five times as large as England, Wales, Scotland and Ireland all put together. The single state of Texas contains territory enough to make two such countries as would be composed jointly of these four, and there would then be enough left to make a State as large as

Virginia, another as large as New Jersey and there would yet be some left.

The joint population of these four countries is 26,123,400 which is a fraction over 225 to the square mile. Were the whole United States settled that thickly instead of a population of 30,000,000 we should have one of over 662,000,000. Or were they settled as thickly as Belgium, which I believe is the most densely populated country on the globe, 326 to the square mile, instead of having a population of 30,000,000 we would have one of over 957,000,000. By these figures we may see that the United States had only made a beginning towards developing her vast resources.

The area of the Territories is considerably over twelve times as large as those four countries taken together, and yet upon all this immense track of country there is only 92,298 inhabitants if we except the Indians; or which is about one inhabitant for every sixteen square miles. There is much of this land very fertile, some of which, I have understood, will produce as much as forty bushels of wheat per acre, and yet it remains there idle and uncultivated, we having more than we can occupy.

These lands for a few years past have been settling up very fast. Before this war commenced about 500,000 emigrants came annually from Europe, a large portion of which settled in these Territories.

Some years ago Congress passed an act giving large amounts of these lands as bounties to the soldiers of the war of 1812 and Mexican war. About the time these lands were being taken up by these soldiers, I made a calculation to see how long it would take at that rate to take them all up, and I found that it would take a little over two hundred years. So under ordinary circumstances it will, I presume, take considerably over two hundred years to take them all up, and even then they would be but thinly settled. From this you can draw some idea of the vast extent of the old United States.

The means of transportation were generally lacking for developing this immense section of the west, and so in January 1861, Congress, I believe, passed a bill for two railroads to the Pacific Ocean, as follows:

Northern Route.—Northern prong to start from the Iowa border. Southern prong to start from a point on the Missouri border, they were to come together in running about two hundred miles, and were to run thence for Sanfrancisco.

Southern Route.—Northern prong to start from fort Smith in Arkansas; Southern prong from a point on the western border of Louisianna. They too, I believe were to unite in running about two hundred miles, and were to run thence for Sanfrancisco. The roads were to be finished in fifteen years. These roads finished would have tended much towards developing this immense section, and bringing these lands into market. The United States had but to speak a thing, as it were, and it was done. Can we cast our eye into the future and see what the United States were destined to have been two or three hundred years hence, all things working together well.

But if the two sections succeed in getting apart, is there any certainty of these Pacific rail roads ever being built. Or should they succeed in getting apart is there any certainty that we will have but two Confederacies. The two sections are now held together by this war, so that there is now no time for subdividing, &c., but let peace be made and mind you if there do not other questions arise that will result in divisions. Some will

want free trade, others a high tariff; some will be for
importing wild Africans, others will oppose it, and
some will be for this thing, and some for that. And
there are the Territories too that will probably be a
fruitful source for dissensions. Let us therefore if possible avoid these divisions by sticking together and
laboring to remedy the defects in our government.

To prove that it is dangerous thus to split up and
divide, I refer the reader to Germany. After a thousand years of destructive civil wars, did she come out
with only two or three Confederacies? No. She count-
ed upwards of three hundred distinct and independent
principalities, each one liable to be conquered by the
nearest despotic government that saw proper to do so.
And if this war should continue for any length of time
have we any assurance that these United States will not
eventually be split up into as many separate divisions
as was Germany. For we have a Territory a good many times as large as Germany, and can therefore better
afford such a split. I will here remark that I examined
my map in order to tell how many times larger the
United States are than Germany. But I found the
country split up into so many small divisions, the sizes
of many of which were not given, so that I was not
able to make the calculation. We must therefore content ourselves by saying that the United States are a
great many times as large as Germany. But should
the United States be eventually divided into that many
separate divisions who is it that does not say in that
event, the country would be ruined. There would then
in all probability be no more rail roads built. Those
Pacific rail roads would probably never be built and
therefore much of our western territory lie unoccupied
and undeveloped for ages to come. Each military

chieftain would probably start and head a faction. Internal strifes would be common, and probably the people here among us, at no distant day, get to cutting off each others heads. The cultivation of the soil would be neglected; because the people would know that if they made any thing, bands of robbers would probably take it away from them. Bands of such men would probably be roving through the country for plunder. No regard whatever would be had for human life. And under these circumstances, desolation and ruin would soon over spread the land. It seems impossible that such should befall our once happy country, but time, the sword and internal dissensions will certainly accomplish the thing if the three hang together long enough. Destroy our civil institutions and let all slip into the hands of the military and we will soon see where it will end. We have the examples of Greece, Rome, the Spanish American Republics, Mexico and others to look at, and when we are following exactly in the same footsteps, what better can we hope for if we thus keep on? They were by nature as wise and intelligent probably as we are. But they destroyed their civil and moral institutions, and as a consequence fell into a state of anarchy and ruin, from which it seems they can never take a rise. Let us then change our course ere we fall into the same deplorable condition, and the canker worm, dissension, sap our institutions to the very foundation.

CHAPTER XIII.

PLAN OF ADJUSTMENT.

I will now end this important subject after first giving my opinion as to what I think we had best do under these trying times. I am under the solemn conviction my countrymen, for the reasons already given, and for reasons that I will hereafter give, that the best thing we can do under the circumstances—the best for ourselves, for our country, and for the rising generation, is to go back into the Union, under the old stars and stripes, and there labor for a reconstruction of the government upon a basis such as shall be as endurable as time itself. Let us not in a rash and evil hour throw away that that cost our forefathers so much, and for which they labored so long and so hard to build up. Let us therefore cast aside the acts of the past, and if possible join together, the North and the South, as erring brothers in reconstructing this great and powerful country, I think it will be to our interest so to do, both for ourselves and for posterity, for time and for eternity. Le us try the thing once more together, and should time prove that we can't live well together, let us then call a convention and separate peaceably, there is no need of having fighting about it.

If we, the people of the North and South, separate by force of arms, we may expect frequently to have contentions that will probably result in wars. If they took our servants when at peace, what will they do when the sections become hostile, or rather have a lasting hostility towards each other? Take still more and give up none will be about the way of it. The extreme Southern States would lose but very few if any by it, but the border Slave States all. The border States would thus be acting as a shield and buckler to the more Southern. This reminds me of a circumstance that took place with Captain John Smith in the early settlement of Virginia.

Whilst out hunting upon a certain occasion Smith was assailed by a party of two hundred Indians, who poured upon him a continual flight of arrows. He seizing one of the assailants, tied him with his garter to his arm and thus used him as a shield to arrest the darts of the enemy. In this way the border slave States have acted and will probably continue to act as a shield to the more Southern, and it was thus being situated I presume that caused them to be so fearless of the result of secession, hence their great desire to embark into it. They knew that they had some one between them and the fire as it were. It seems that they embarked into this secession move and from that to the war without counting the cost. People commencing such a work as this should, I think always count the cost to see whether or not it will pay, and if they have sufficient means to finish. As the Scriptures somewhere say.

"For which of you intendinding to build a tower siteth not down first and counteth the cost whether he have sufficient to finish, lest happily after he hath laid the foundation and is not able to finish, all that behold it begin to mock him saying, this man began to build and was not able to finsh." So of secession. Those states that were so desirous of seceding before doing so should I think, first have had the best mathematicians of the day engaged for weeks calculating to see whether or not such a course would pay.

All I think will now doubtless admit, that thus far we have lost a great deal more by secession and the war than we have gained by them, and there is a probability if this war continue any length of time of still losing a great deal more, both in property and lives, making our condition a great deal worse than what it now is or ever has been—irrevocably bad.

I wish here to introduce our young friend Charley and finish the comparison that I was making between him and the seceded states when we last dismissed him.

We saw that he was in water in which he could not swim; that he was using great exertions and thereby exhausting himself; that he was also in the act of drowning and but for timely aid, and a restoration to his natural element, land, that he soon would have drowned.

So with these states that have seceded. It is evident that their conditions is growing worse every day. But still they hang on to this watery element, that I may term it into which they have plunged. So why hang on in this way when it is evident that we will drown as a nation in another twelve month, unless we learn this great art—swimming—and thus cross over this difficult stream, unto which we have committed ourselves. And how can we learn when there are persons continually discharging missiles at us whilst thus in the water? They are willing to help us out, but because we won't consent to come out they are throwing every obstacle that they possibly can in our way to make our swimming still more difficult, and thus force us to come out. Now I think we have tried it in this new element long enough to find out that we can't swim whilst this other party is so busily engaged discharging missiles at us and using their utmost exertions to frustrate our designs, and are determined it seems, if possible, either to destroy us, or compell us to forsake this new element. I therefore think we had best consent to go out on our natural element, land, and try it there again once more, for we have, like Charley, exerted ourselves to such a degree in this watery element, that I now have no idea that we could walk as well upon land as we did before, even were we now upon it. A half loaf though is better than no bread and better in my opinion go·maimed than not go at all. We have already expended much treasure in this new element as well as lost many valuable lives. And though we can't now walk so well upon land as we could before embarking in this new element the probability is, that by some rest and rubbing down and anointing, that the remainder of us would soon get so as to be able to walk pretty tolerably well. Let us therefore go out and stay out at least long enough to make an agreement with this other party that should we conclude to try this new element again, that they will not discharge any missiles at us whilst in the water, but let us depart in peace.

Under all these considerations, I think it will be best to go back into the Union and try it there once more. If we could use any means to get those large armies disbanded and return home, it would then I presume,· be hard to get them in the field again, both the North and the South.

This generation now knows something of war, and if they ever get out of the one that they are now in, they will I presume take more pains in the future to avoid a war.

Notwithstanding history was open to us and described the many hardships, privations and sufferings that our forefathers endured to achieve our liberties, how they even marched over frozen ground barefooted, and left their footprints behind, stained with blood that ran from their bleeding feet, yet it would not all do for this generation. They had to learn a lesson by practical experience: Wars, I think are frequently looked on too much as a frolic. Many persons, I think, and particularly inexperienced youths, frequently draw vivid hopes of earthly honor and glory to be won on a battle field, which are never realized, and instead thereof they frequently experience hardships, suffering and sometimes death. The glory that one can win on a battle field, I think, rightly considered, is of but short duration. We should not be too ready to go to war. See 40.

Do you suppose our forefathers, had they have been here, would have disrupted the Union for the causes that existed at the beginning of our sectional troubles? No never, never. A voice from our dead that had fallen in the achievement of our liberties, and who now lay mouldering in a common grave, would have come up before them saying, down with your scisms and divisions. It is not for this that we fought, bled and died. Keep united and you will be a great, prosperous and happy people.

Therefore, I think we had best go back into the old Union and try it there under the stars and stripes once more. It may be bad if we go back, we don't doubt that at all. In all probability it will be a great deal worse with us for many years to come, whether we go back in the Union or not, than it would have been had we not seceded; but we now can't help this. The two evils are now upon us. Some people it seems could not be satisfied until they brought them upon us, and we must now get out of them the best way we can. Though it be bad for us to go back into the Union, it may still be a great deal worse for us not to go back; so of the two evils, let us choose the less. "How long halt ye between two opinions."

Some may argue that it will not do to go back in the

Union; that the North will make us pay all the expenses. I will here remark that I consider one human life alone worth more than all the property in the Northern and Southern States; our first object should therefore be to save human life as much as possible. I therefore think it a bad plan to estimate the value of human life by dollars and cents. But do we know that the North would thus be for our paying all the expenses? By settling the difficulty by a compromise the business may probably be arranged in quite a different way—perhaps by each party paying their own cost, or else by casting both debts together and making one immense national debt of the two, but if we have to be driven back, I then don't know how it may be. I therefore think the sooner a compromise is struck for the better.

We have, I presume public lands enough in the United States if sold at a fair value to nearly or quite pay the public debt. But just think of it, should our lands even pay this debt, that we will then have expended in this war a sum as large, as a fertile country more than twelve times as large as England, Wales, Scotland and Ireland all put together, will sell for.

We have public lands enough in the territories at the low price of two dollars per acre to amount to the astounding sum of $1,884,238,080. That with what we have in the State of Florida, together with that in other new States would, I presume swell the amount to quite $2,000,000,000.

There is much of these lands worth instead of two dollars, more than twenty dollars per acre; some of which I have understood will produce forty bushels of wheat per acre.

How then will we ever get any of these lands or the proceeds itself unless we go back into the Union? The

North being vastly superior as to numbers we would stand but a bad chance to undertake to fight them out of them.

Although the people at the North have said and done a great deal to keep slavery out of the Territories, they had not as yet I believe, done any thing to keep us from receiving our distributive share of the proceeds arising from the sale of these lands. We will say that we were likely not to get our rights in the Territories, that is, not permitted to carry our servants there and settle, we got our distributive share of the money arising from the sale of these lands, and as for territory we already had enough of that to do ourselves and servants too for many generations to come; yes we will say for thousands of years to come. Then why be so ready to create a disturbance about that that we can never enjoy. But I am not for thus easily surrendering our rights to these lands. I think a fair way to divide these lands would be to do so according to the ratio of population between the North and the South and according to the area of land now embraced in each section. In order that I may be understood I will endeavor to make this some plainer. We will put down the population of the Nort at 20,000,000; that of the South at 10,000,000. The area of the Northern States embrace 612,597 square miles, or 392,062,080 acres. This divided by 20,000,000, will give nearly twenty acres to each inhabitant at the North.

The area of the Southern States embrace 851,508 square miles, or 544,965,120 acres. This divided by 10,000,000 will give a little over fifty-four acres to each inhabitant at the South. So before dividing the Territories the North should, I think be made up, or have thirty-four acres thrown in to each inhabitant, so as to make her count fifty-four acres of land to each inhabitant. Then divide the balance according to population, which would be to give the North two acres and the South one. Let us see how this calculation will figure. 20,000,000 people to have each thirty-four acres of land, to make them equal to the South, will amount to 680,000,000 acres, or 1,002,500 square miles, this amount taken from 1,492,061 square miles—what is embraced in the Territories, will leave 409,561 square miles to be divided between the North and the South. One third of this is 136,520 square miles—the portion of the South—nearly three times as large as North Carolina. If we could get a country of that size out of the Territories to carry our servants to and settle, or in other words, if we could add three States of about the size of North Carolina to the slave States, and then get our distributive share of the proceeds arising from the sale of the balance of these lands, I think we could then afford to settle the territorial question.

But it may be argued that this division should be made according to the ratio of population soon after the revolution, that these Territories were then common property, and that we should not wait this long until the Northern States have been settled up largely by foreigners, and has thus given them a great advantage over us if we now divide according to the ratio of population. I will admit that there is some feasibility in such an argument. But at the same time we do not need all the Territory that would thus accrue to us, to carry our servants to. And I do not see any use in acting the dog in the manger. We can't occupy and settle these lands ourselves and I see no use in placing an impediment in the way to keep others from settling them. This Continent may have been intended by the

All wise Creator for the purpose for which it now seems to be so well adapted—an asylum for the crowded and miserably poor of the Eastern Continent, and I therefore think we should not throw any obstacles in the way of its settlement. Our forefathers sought an asylum here where they might rest at ease, and I now think we should extend the same hand of fellowship to our fellow man.

As the Northern States, owing to the tide of emigration have increased in numbers much faster than we have, there is a probability of their eventually wanting more Territory upon which to settle, or wanting it at least in proportion to their present numbers.

But it may be argued that these lands should be divided according to the Federal population soon after the close of the revolution, and had we have chosen to make free States of a portion of them we could do so, but let the proceeds thereof come exclusively to the Southern States. This would have been fair had the division been made soon after that time, but the way it now is, I don't know if it would not be as fair, taking every thing into consideration, to divide them according to Federal population after the plan mentioned, and the proceeds thereof in the same way, or apply them to the expenses of general government, the way they have generally been applied.

If we thus had enough of these Territories laid off to make three such States as North Carolina, the portion of these Territories that would then fall to the North, though nearly ten times as large as ours, would in all probability be settled up first. I don't think it any advantage either to the slaves, or slave holders to scatter them over so much country—but rather the reverse. Therefore, I think if we could get enough of these Ter-

ritories to make three States about the size of North
Carolina, or more exactly 136,520 square miles, and
then get our distributive share of the proceeds of the
balance that this part of the question would be settled
fairly and equitably. I can't see how it is any worse
for a servant to cultivate an acre of land in these Territories than it is in any other part of the Southern or
United States, and while such a course does not propose
to increase the number of servants, I can't tell how it
can increase the evil. As this territorial question is one
fraught with so many troubles and dangers to our well
being, I think it should be settled and settled forever;
either by running a line east and west, and give the
South the Southern portion, or should the North object
to thus dividing it, and giving to the south all the Southern portion, run the line north and south so as to give to
each section a variety of climate. Establish this line
either east and west, or north and south, as the case may
be, and let it be done permanently. Have no more
voting upon it.

At these elections when a State is to be admitted into the Union with or without slavery, as the people
may say, there is always too much excitement at them,
too apt to be blood spilt. But have the territories devided so that if any one is desirous of removing to them
with his servants, he knows where to go—and if he is
desirous of going to a free State he also knows where to
go? Fixed in this way, the North would then have some
the advantage, because one can come from the free
States and settle and live in a slave State just as well
as if he had come from a slave State, and if he is afterwards desirous of doing so, he can buy servants and
live there with the same privileges as though he had
been a Southern man out and out. But if a Southern

man goes to a free State, he has to leave his servants, if he has any, behind. In this the North has some the advantage, but let us not fall out about that. There is no need of falling out about it, for both sections would then have territory enough to do them for thousands and thousands of years to come. In order to show our greedy disposition, I will use the following illustrations: You may offer a child an apple, he will take it in his hand; offer him another, he will take that in the other hand; offer him a third and having no place for it, he will commence crying about it. So with us about our public lands. We already have about as much as we can occupy, and there still being a large amount unoccupied, we must have a great contention about that, when the probability is that they will not be occupied for many generations to come. I don't, though advise being prodigal with these lands because we have a super-abundance of them, but I think the fact that there is such a vast amount of them, should induce each party to yield so as to settle the territorial question fairly and peaceably, and without any disturbance. Each party would then, I think, have as much land as they would ever know what to do with. This I think would be a fair plan to settle upon, fair and just to both parties, I may say. Because at the formation of the Constitution of the United States, there were but thirteen States, twelve of which were slave holding. In time the people of the Northern States sold their servants to the people of the Southern States. Even Connecticut tolerated slavery as late as the year 1840. The territories were then joint stock, and I can't see why the people of the Southern States should forfeit their right to settle in these territories merely because they bought the servants of the northern people.

The institution of slavery has now got a foothold with us and I now don't know what better we can do with them than to keep them and treat them well, and if it be wrong let it between us and our God. If it be wrong I presume the people at the north will have a portion of the sin to answer for, because they sold theirs into bondage. I will here remark before quitting this subject that I am very desirous of seeing laws passed for the general good treatment of servants in order that neither the north, nor any one else, can have ought to say against us concerning that matter. I have reasons for speaking as I have respecting the treatment of servants, which I will make known at the proper place.

CHAPTER XIV.

PLAN OF ADJUSTMENT CONTINUED.

THE RIGHTEOUS SHOULD RULE.

Should it eventually turn out that the Southern Confederacy will stand, or that the seceded States will have to go back into the Union, I think in either case, it should be put into the Constitution that none but religious, pious persons should be eligible to office from that of Clerk and Sheriff up to the President of the United States. There is no irreligious man that will make a good officer who would not make a better one were he a professor of religion. The Bible, I think says, " When the wicked rule the people mourn, but when the righteous rule the people rejoice." The Bible I think gives conclusive evidence that righteous persons make the best rulers. God, that made the world can, I think, best govern it, and that a righteous person comes nearer being a vicegerent of God than a wicked person is evident.

A wicked man is scarcely fit to govern a family, let alone a nation of people. He lacks that calmness and serenity of temper which bears him up in the hour of trial and trouble.

Religion to a man is what the regulator is to a steam engine, it causes him to take an even and a regular course, through life—like a ship at sea in time of a storm. She does not mount upon every wave as a frail light bark would do, but plows through them and thus keeps on an even and direct course. The ship having ballast enables her to do thus. Religion then to a man is what ballast is to a ship, it causes him to take an even course through life's uneven way. Religious persons will evidently make the best officers, but how often do we see the wicked thrust into power as it were, when the more modest, less assuming and more religious are left out.

Some may object to thus mixing state and clergy; but suppose all the people throughout the land were righteous. That we had no wicked persons from which to select our politicians, and as a consequence none but religious persons were elected to office, don't you think we would soon have very different times from what we have had? If we had had such men to fill our offices for the last fifty years, we would not now, I presume have this horrible civil war upon us. If all persons were religious we should not now, I presume have any use for those large guns and other munitions of war now being made and used with which to destroy the lives of our fellow man. We have plenty of room for them all for many generations to come. No need of killing up any. When we consider the large number of human beings slain in wars and that otherwise die, we may truly say that wars are deplorable evils. Our young men (both sections) had better in my opinion prepare to fill some useful station in life, to administer aid and comfort to their afflicted fellow man, and wait God's own appointed time to die, than thus needlessly to throw away their lives in wicked wars. Are our soldiers that fall in battle prepared for this great change? They should remember that in the next world they have an eternity to live. Being slain' in battle alone is not going to save them, though they be upon the right side. They must first have been born again, and have faith in Jesus Christ, before they may expect to reap the joys of another world.

As has been already remarked a truly pious ruler approaches nearer a vicegerent of God, than any other person we can possibly select, and that government in the hands of such men approaches nearest a Theocracy, such as was before king Saul commenced to reign, is also evident. Then let us approximate a Theocracy as near as possible by making our officers and rulers exclusively of pious men.

There is probably no position in our country that calls for good pious men more, or that needs their services worse, than does the various offices of our country, from that of Clerk, Sheriff, &c., up to the Presidency of the United States. And whether we succeed in building up this Southern Confederacy, or whether we go back to the old Union, let us do this thing—put only good pious men at the head of government affairs, and put it in the Constitution "that none others but such shall be put there." I will here remark that it should not be men of superficial piety only that should hold the offices of our country, but the genuine professors—

men who have had their hearts changed. Our government placed in the hands of such men, I think, would stand the shock of ages, and until this be done, I don't think we can ever have a permanent governtment. I think it is already clearly enough demonstrated that the wicked are incapable of self government without ever trying that experiment again.

But the good effect, that elevating exclusively to the offices of our country, pious men is not the only good effect that such a course, I think, would have. Religion would be encouraged, and by this means the good tidings of great joy would probably soon be proclaimed, with a more saving effect throughout the length and breadth of our entire land, and the gladsome news, that the dead is alive, the lost is found, be thus sent home to the heart of many a poor sinner. A great part of our sinful population might thus probaby soon be brought "their Redeemer to know." Joy would then spring up in every corner of the land, and peace and contentment reign throughout the entire length and breadth thereof.

You will please pardon me for saying here, that I believe such a course as the above would have a great effect on religion; that it would probably cause many persons to become professors who never do, because I don't think religion would then be viewed in the persecuted light in which it is now generally viewed; there would be more inducements to seek after it, (pardon me here) and we have the promise that those that seek shall find, and after finding their great regret is that they had not sought and obtained sooner. Having somewhat digressed from the subject, I will now return to it again.

I will now soon end this important subject, after first summing up what I conceive to be a fair basis for the

North and South to settle upon. I herewith submit it.

1 Let the South pass laws for the better treatment of servants according to the plan already given.

2 Let the North repeal those personal liberty bills.

3 Establish the Missouri Compromise line, or some other line as already mentioned and thus give the South equal rights in the Territories.

4 Respect the fugitive slave law.

5 Let the South pass laws such as would protect her manufacturing interest according to plan already given.

6 Insert in the Constitution that none but pious, religious persons should be eligible to office.

7 Let all go back into the Union and be good clever fellows, and let the experience of the past be a lesson for the future.

8 Permit all to come back to the Union with the rights and privileges of citizens as though there had been no war. Let there be no farther sacrifice of life or property on either side.

9 As regards the expenses of the war, let each side pay its own expense, or else cast both debts together and make a joint National debt.

Before quiting this important subject, I must urge once more upon my Southern brethren the importance of putting a stop to this cruel war by going back into the Union. I do so through love and veneration for them, believing it, under the circumstances, the best thing that we can now do, and I think I have a right to know some of these things, which I will relate at the proper place. I desire to see no farther sacrifice of human life, neither on the part of the North nor the South. If this war should continue any length of time, there is a probability of the mortality caused by it, equaling, if not exceeding, that of the French revolution. During that terribie civil war, there were over 1,000,000 human beings slain, over 1,800 of which were beheaded with the guillotine, (a machine for the purpose, that cuts off a head at a single stroke.)

I will here remark, that the population of France and that of the United States is about equal, both being about 30,000,000. Should we lose a million of men in this terrible struggle, mostly the youth of our country, what a dreadful calamity it would be! And as regards futurity, we may, perhaps, say thousands of millions. Of all wars, civil wars are the most disastrous and destructive, both to property and human life; because each side is apt to put forth its entire strength. At the rates that our men (North and South) are now falling, it will not take long, I presume, for its victims to reach even a million. Let us, therefore, hope that our difficulties will soon be settled and the evils of war be removed from this once happy country.

There may be an objection raised to going back into the Union, for the reason that the North will probably be for making us pay the expenses of this war, and will also persecute our citizens. I though don't believe there is any foundation for either of these suppositions. The Democratic party is now largely in the majority at the North and the prospect of things appears to be very unfavorable for such a supposition as the above, for within the last ten months the Democratic party to the North has held State Conventions and nominated full democratic tickets in every free State in the Union.

To prove that this great party is also conservative, and advocates the war on the part of the Federal government, merely for restoring all to the Union again, with equal rights and privileges, I refer the reader to the following extract of an address issued by fourteen prominent Democratic members of the Federal Congress, and which you may find in the North Carolina Standard of June 11th, 1862.

"We scorn to reply to the charge that the Democratic party is opposed to granting aid and support to the Federal Government in maintaining its safety, integrity and Constitutional supremacy, and in favor of disbanding our armies and succombing to the South. The charge is libelous and false. No man has advocated any such proposition. Democrats recognise it as their duty as patriots to support the government in all its constitutional, necessary and proper efforts to maintain its safety, integrity and constitutional authority; but at the same time they are inflexibly opposed to waging a war against any of the states or people of this Union in any spirit of oppression, or for any purpose of conquest or subjugation, or of overthrowing or interfering with the rights or established institutions of any state. Above all, the democratic party will not support the administration in any thing which looks or tends to the loss of our political or personal rights and liberties, or a change of our present democratical form of government."

I have another reason for advocating that the seceded states had best go back into the Union and that is that I don't believe this Southern Confederacy can stand, and that therefore the sooner we go back the better it will be for us, and the less the loss both in lives and property. I have two reasons for thus believing, one of which I will give here, or they may I suppose, 1 e sumed up pretty much in one, the main body of them I will give here, but the why and wherefore, I will retain for another place.

It has already, I think been shown that any of the slave holders at the south may at any time with impunity act, and some of them have acted what should have been unconstitutional in the treatment of their servants. The offense of mistreatment of servants being of longer standing or of more ancient date than these personal liberty bills detracts, I think, from the offensiveness of the latter; these offences then in my opinion about balance. So the south, I think should not have kicked up such a dust at these personal liberty bills, until they themselves had passed some better laws for the treatment of servants, and as this great reform for their better treatment has not yet been made by law, and as this great fuss and disturbance arose principally about them, and taking also into consideration the many unjust means that were resorted to, to bring on general secession—such as lying telegrams, &c. I am inclined to think that this Southern Confederacy can't long stand upon its present foundation.

I was about to close my remarks without citing to Henry Clay on secession, a true patriot and lover of his country, and a man whose worth was not fully appreciated until after he was gone; and though we may not have dealt with him justly in every respect whilst he was with us, it is now too late—he is gone. This circumstance reminds me of a story of a little boy that I once read, who, one night after he had gone to bed, commenced crying. His father asked him what was the matter. Why says he, I recollect upon a certain occasion that my little brother Jimmy wanted my top to play with and I would not let him have it, now he is dead and I can't, and the thought of it filled the little fellow's soul with anguish. So of our sage and hero whether or not we dealt justly with him whilst among us, it is now too late to amend as to that—he is gone. But he has left us his advice upon this all important ubject. Let us see what it is. See 41.

CHAPTER XV.

SUDDEN CALL OF GOD AND PROFESSION OF RELIGION.

My main reasons for believing that this Southern Confederacy can't long stand upon its present foundation, are founded in a profesion of religion, or in things that were made known to me above fourteen years ago, and it is what I then experienced that has caused me to attempt to write the present work. And though there be many things that happened to me at that time that will appear strange to the reader, they are nevertheless true to a pins point, as nigh as I am able to relate them, and I don't think I can be mistaken in any thing, because there was too much power attending their visitation. The visions, revelations, &c., that then appeared unto me, I look upon as the plainest of all things that have taken place during my life, and though above fourteen years ago, I recollect them with the greatest accuracy, and don't think I have forgotten scarcely a jot since.

In order that I may be understood, I will begin back at the beginning and mention probably some of the producing causes. With these introductory remarks, I herewith submit the principal part of these visions and revelations.

In the spring of 1848, I was going to school at Carthage, N. C. I have been both the diligent the neglectful student. During my first schooling I was tolerably apt until I learned Grammar, Geography and Arithmetic. I was then put to Latin, Greek and Geometry. Not having much relish for these studies, particularly the two former, I was dragging in my class for a year or so. At length a circumstance occurred that in no small degree tended to spur me up in my studies. It was this. Our excellent tutor, Rev. A. C. McNeill, talked of quitting the school at Carthage after the close of the then present session, and going to South Carolina to teach there. I then began seriously to reflect on the thing, thinking that after the close of the present session, my opportunities for learning might probably be wound up. The consequence was, I applied myself diligently to my studies. Difficulties began to vanish, and I was soon making fine progress in my studies. Such a spirit seemed generally to have pervaded the school; all the schollars appeared to learn faster. I had passed from a state of gloomy despondency to one of constant delight. I attended closely to my studies, and when I went to recite I generally understood my lessons well, so much so that our excellent, assistant tutor, Mr. Archibald Ray, wished to increase my Latin lesson. I was then getting a page of a night, and could read it almost as fluently as English; but I was conscious that he was not aware of the immense study that it took to get it in that fix, and so objected to it.

I kept two slates, one at my room, the other at the school room, and was practicing writing to a considerable extent, with which to learn these studies, and I thought, with marked benefit too. I had studied to such a degree and pleased with the progress that I was making, that I got so that I could not sleep well of a night, or at least not well in the forepart of the night. I would thus lay awake probably an hour or so thinking on some difficulty in my studies. My mind was continually going. All was pleasure and contentment, or at least, it was rather a pleasure than a burden to me to study. Many times I would thus lay down at night and when I would arise in the morning I would know more about my studies than when I lay down. Upon one occasion feeling somewhat wearied, I went up in my room after dinner and lay down, thinking I would rest a little while, I soon dropped off to sleep and when I awoke the school boys were returning from school. About this time I became ardently attached to a young lady. Each day seemed like my attachment was stronger. Although I had never broached the subject to her, I had resolved to do so at an early day. Circumstances though turned up so as to decree things otherwise. My attachment though for her was so strong that I loved her for years after she was married. I am therefore an advocate of early marriages, although I have not practiced it myself.

Well, feeling somewhat burdened with my studies, I resolved going up home and spending a few days fishing with a hook and line, an exercise of which I was very fond; I accordingly went up on Wednesday or Thursday, intending to return to my school again on Sunday. I then lacked one day of being eighteen years old. I remarked to a friend at Carthage, before leaving, that "to-day I can't muster, but to-morrow I can," meaning that I would then be eighteen years old. Little did I think what would take place before that time should arrive.

I will here remark that the Friday after I left was composition day, it being a custom of the school to write and hand in one every two weeks. I had accordingly written mine and sent it in the day I left by one of the students. Whether or not it could be considered a good one, it was one upon which I had bestowed a good deal of labor. I closed it with the first three or four verses of the xiv. chap. of St. John. Well, that evening I went on home and got there about dusk. During the evening I had a good deal of conversation with my father and step-mother.

After a while bed time came on and I went up stairs to bed by myself. My two brothers and step-brother had gone a fishing—striking with a torch and gig. Well, soon after laying down I commenced studying on another composition that I intended writing out by our next composition day. I was going to describe a battle between Pluto, the god of the infernal regions, and the God of heaven. I had before given this subject much study, and was now studying on it with great intensity of mind. I had it about ready for the pen, so that when I went to write it I would have had but little to do more than write it off as fast as I could write. It was to be an ærial battle, or one fought in the air, and in substance pretty much as follows :

All the powers of hell were to be mustered against those of heaven. It was to be a decisive battle. If Pluto and his army whipped there would be no more heaven, and if God and his army whipped there would be no more hell. God and his army were to be mounted on white steeds, clad in white apparel, with scarlet caps and a bright star in front. Pluto and his army were to be mounted on black steeds, clad in black apparel, and to have the appearance of death. Both armies being ready at a given signal they strike a lope to join battle. They soon join. The battle now rages fierce and heavy, and nothing can be heard but the loud clanking and jarring of warlike instruments and the fruitless cries on the side of Pluto and his men for mercy. The battle rages still fiercer and heavier, and there is a prospect of Pluto and his men soon being utterly discomfited and *his power forever overthrown. At this moment God in person attacks Pluto and succeeds in unhorsing him. He then dismounts to use him up with his sword.

As I was about this point, my mind intensely engaged with the closing scenes of the imaginary battle, all at once a light flashed across the top of the room just like lightning. The streams appeared to be about two or three inches across and two or three in number. In a second or so after the first flash, it flashed a second time. It was, according to my recollection, perfectly fair, or at least I have no idea that this lightning came from a cloud. In a second or so after the second flash I saw an Image stand before me, the brightest thing that I had ever seen in all my life. I saw it when it was about two feet high and it kept getting higher and higher until it got to be about the size of a man. I had never seen anything that would begin to compare with it for brightness. I not expecting to see any such a thing was frightened, and thinking of Moses, veiled my face unable to behold the glory thereof. In a few seconds there was an influence that moved over me, such as dispeled this fear. I then uncovered my face and would have been glad to have seen this bright Image, or rather perhaps person of God, again, but it was gone. From the first though, I felt as if it was no common work that was upon me. I now heard an alarm watch, such as I had frequently heard belonging to Capt. Daniel McKethan; this was the only watch that I ever recollect seeing that would give an alarm at a desired hour; it made a noise more like the singing of a rattlesnake than anything I can compare it to. The noise that I now heard seemed to be exactly like that, so much so that it appeared the two could not have been told apart. It was made known to me what it was for —to alarm me that time was near, or precious, and I should be a doing.

I next heard a popping and a burning as of a great fire. I could distinctly hear the singing of twigs or thistles as plainly as I ever heard them in a new ground when on fire—such as sing out of brush heaps. There were next some things made known to me not necessary to mention here, I therefore omit them.

I felt a weight on my breast as if there had been a fifty pound weight there; this I suppose was sin, and I believe began by degrees to be removed.

God now began to make known to me my duty or things that he wished me to accomplish.

It was revealed to me that the object of my call was that the plan of salvation might be enlarged. It was revealed to me that the plan already fixed was thought to be sufficient to save the whole human family, but still numbers and numbers kept passing on down to hell. The plan as amended was to embrace the whole human family—all were to be saved.

It was also represented to me that owing to oaths which the Lord had taken and which had to be respected, that it was a hard and difficult thing to do that he had been looking for a suitable person to call to this work, and had at length chosen me for that purpose. It was also told me why I was chosen, and why at the age of eighteen. The reason that I was chosen, at eighteen was because it was the age at which the Jews married; why this shouldh ave any thing to do with it I am now unable to tell. There was also one other reason given why I was called to this work, but which I will not give in this narrative.

Another reason was, my having been of a sad morose

disposition had induced me to trouble, and it had to be
a person that had experienced trouble. My mind having broken the fetters of sadness through the exhilarating effects of books and passionate love, seemed to fit me for the arduous undertaking. There was another thing that had a great effect on my mind in producing lively hopes and expectations, and which I should have mentioned sooner. When at school at Carthage, by swinging a watch chain, I was led to an idea by which I believed I had discovered perpetual motion. I had resolved to test it by experiment in the coming vacation of the school, but I have never yet tested it, and so can't tell whether or not it will work. The thought though of having discovered it had a very exhilarating effect on my mind. Having somewhat digressed from the subject, I will now return to it again.

It will be impossible to convey a just idea of the many powerful truths that were made known to me during this eventful night. About this time my two brothers and step brother, who had been fishing, came in. They not having been in my company much for some time, wished to knock up a chat with me, and Aaron, my eldest brother, asked me if I did not want to clerk it for Colonel Hancock at Carthage. I told him no, not for forty dollars per month. He appeared a good deal surprised at this, and wanted to know the reason; I told him I would tell him the meaning of all this at some future period. The boys seeing I did not want to talk with them, soon dropped off to sleep. These revelations and visions still kept on with me.

Some time during the night I had a vision of hell as plain a thing as I ever saw. I could see it perfectly plain over to my left of a green or bluish color. I was then laying on my left side. It was revealed to me that

if I would lay a little longer I could hear the shrieks
and wails of human beings therein; but I was so shock-
ed at what I had already seen that I turned over to
keep from seeing any more. These things kept on with
me all night. If I slept any it was but little. I probably slept a little from about day light to sun up or
there about. I can't though say positively that I slept,
or that I did not sleep. Any how when I got up and
went down stairs every thing looked new and changed.
I though as well as I recollect, did not tell the family of
any of these things that had taken place the night before. I don't think I had any thing to say to any of
them. Notwithstanding I had been awake the most if
not all of the night previous, I did not feel sleepy in the
least. I felt easy and contented and across my peace-
ful breast not a wave of trouble rolled. The change
that I felt had taken place I believe I should have taken
for religion, had I experienced no greater change. I
was though still under Divine influence; still being led
on as it were. After awhile breakfast came on and I
was asked in. I set down at the table but I did not
feel hungry. They had fish for breakfast. I told them
I would eat some fish in remembrance, but I do not
think I told them in remembrance of what, but I meant
Christ performing miracles with the loaves and fishes.
I ate but a few mouthfuls when I got up and went out
and lay down on a bench in the piazza, Seemed like
as I went the sun shown with uncommon brilliancy, or
with a soft silvery light, such as I had never before
witnessed. Although I was laying in the sunshine, it
appeared to be the best and most comfortable place that
I ever had been in, in all my life. The first one that
came out to me was my youngest brother, Benjamin, a
child some two years old I presume, or just beginning

paddle about. He came and rubed his hands over my vest buttons; it caused me to love that child better than I can tell, and this circumstance causes me still to look upon him with tender regard. My father and step mother soon came out and desired me to go in and lay down on a bed, as I was laying in the sunshine; but I thought it was the best place that I ever had been in and so refused to go. About this time my two little sisters were engaged with a wheel in the farther end of the piazza, spinning, twisting thread or something of the sort, and whilst thus engaged they sang a song, called the Millennium.

I know I thought it was the prettiest song I ever had heard in all my life, and seemed like it was sung on purpose for me. My father and the balance of the family kept insisting on my going in out of the sun. I had no notion of going and therefore their talking to me only tended to confuse me. Whilst there, there came a little sparrow near me on the floor. My step mother remarked that there was a little bird with a sore foot. I cast my eye down and saw that one of its feet was drawn up as though it had been burnt.

This was now the 29th day of March, and about nine or ten o'clock in the day. The cocks crowed a good deal, and it seemed to be impressed on me that a new day was about to dawn. Some would crow and not finish their notes, stopping about half way. It was afterwards told me what this was for, which I will probably relate at the proper place, should I take my narrative that far. The reason that I suppose it to be about nine or ten o'clock in the day is, that I have since noticed at that time of the year and at that time of day the cocks are apt to take a spell at crowing. Well my people finding that I was not going in of my own accord

laid hands on me to bear me in. Seemed like as s[oon]
as they touched me for this purpose my breath sto[pped]
and I became stiff and cold as a dead person. See[med]
like I was dead and felt so except about my heart
joyful wheels of life still went on. It seems to m[e I]
did not draw my breath the first time whilst they w[ere]
thus bearing me. But I was soon to be restored.
they laid me down on a bed I awoke as it were on
beds of Paradise, and never felt so joyful and happy
all my life. I felt that my sins, which were man[y]
were all forgiven, and I shouted and praised God w[ith]
all the power that I was master of, and then could [not]
praise him half enough. The joy that one feels
having his sins all forgiven is such as no one can dr[aw]
any idea of, except it be by those that have experienc[ed]
it, and is such as none can tell. I looked with wond[er]
and astonishment how I had staid away from so go[od]
a Being so long. I was eighteen years old that ve[ry]
day, and saw, I think, more real pleasure and satisfa[c]
tion in that one day, than I had seen in the balance [of]
my life. I had a universal love for the whole hum[an]
family, and for my relatives at home I felt particula[rly]
concerned. I told my father and step mother that [I]
would have them or knock down hell's door, meani[ng]
that I would follow them to that awful place before [I]
would give them up. I think though that it was
some subsequent time when I had been greatly wroug[ht]
upon, that I told them this.

It would now seem that after I had professed religio[n]
my travel might be over, but not so. Many deep an[d]
mysterious truths were now made known to me. Man[y]
things were now revealed to me by lessons as it wer[e.]
After one of these lessons had been revealed to me, [I]
would have an irresistible desire to arise and proclai[m]

the family. I spake as I had never before spoken. [Se]emed like the words were put in my mouth as fast [as] I could utter them. During the course of these re[]lations I was led through deep and mysterious things, [an]d when I looked back and saw the great difficulties [th]at I had been led through, it appeared to me, that [ha]d I have known at the start the many difficulties that had to go through, that I could never have held out. [B]ut by their being presented to me one at a time, I [wa]s at length led through. There was nothing com[pu]lsory as regards my duty that I know of; but it all [was left] to my choice which to pursue—the part of Godli[ne]ss or not. I invariably choose the part by which I [th]ought I might keep in favor of God, and by which [th]e object for which I was called might be best ac[co]mplished.

At length after some days, the work appeared to be [sett]led, and it seemed that I would do for this important [wo]rk. How long this was from the time of my first [cal]l I am not now able to tell, but I am inclined to [thi]nk that it was not longer than three or four days. [But] the time though longer or shorter it at length ap[pe]ared to be all through, and that I would answer for [hi]s great purpose. But it seemed necessary in order [th]at this work might be fulfilled that I should go to [he]aven in order that my mission might be completed. [S]o it was revealed to me one day in the day time that [Go]d would send down his angels that night for the pur[po]se of carrying me to heaven. I was willing to go. [Th]ere were two doors to the room in which I lay; one [wa]s a back door opening out into the yard; the other [ope]ning into a hall. I wanted the angels to come in [at t]he hall door. I had my fears about the back door; [see]med like it was a door of death or devils or some[thi]ng so, and in order that they might not come in at that door, I had a servant boy of the name of Spencer to make him down a pallet across the door and lay there. I will remark here that I lay by myself after the first night of my call. Well I was laying awake and I think about ten o'clock, I heard several raps at this back door, as though some one had raped with their knuckles. I without hesitation said no entrance to devils there; they then raped a second time, I said the same words, and I heard no more of them that night. There was nothing more of interest that I recollect of that transpired during the night.

I believe it was the next night that I had another chance of going to heaven. The room appeared to be filled with soft light, and had I been willing, it appeared that I would have gone upward. I was willing to go but first wanted the 4th seal which was the one directly over card playing. I had, when a neglectful student at Carthage, lost much of my time card-playing when I should have been at my studies, and so I first wanted that seal. But in consequence of my not going in the way that it seemed pleasing to God that I should go, this fell through. I will hear remark that there were eight seals, but, the uses of all I dont think had been fully made known to me. The fourth from this circumstance was impressed on my mind, and is still retained.

I believe it was the next night I was tried again. I was laying on the bed by myself, and the first thing I knew, I saw a bright Image alight suddenly on a bureau that was standing near a window. After remaining there a few moments it suddenly went out through the window. As it went, my head was raised up off of the bed and drawn after it so as to make a bow, or my obeisance, to it as it went. Presently it came back and sat about the same place. In a few seconds it went out again. In the meantime it had been told me what it was for, to see if I would bow to it of my own accord as I had been shown; I accordingly bowed as I had been shown as near as I could. In a few seconds it came in again, and came and sat apparently on the head board a foot or two above my head, and shown down on me seem like with the brightness of the sun. It was made known to me that by laying as I was and letting it shine on me, the necessary power would be given me. It seems I had refused two opportunities of going to heaven, and now the necessary means were brought directly to me. I reflected that I was young; that older and perhaps more deserving persons had never had such an opportunity offered them; Franklin for one I know crossed my mind. So out of affected modesty, little thinking of the consequences, I refused this also, and covered my head to keep it from shining on me.

I will here remark that this Image, person of God, or whatever it was, did not appear to be larger than a man from his shoulders up, and scarcely so broad across the base. It appeared to be of the same brightness of the Image, or rather perhaps person of God, that I had seen at the beginning of those memorable scenes. I will also state that one reason that I refused to let this Image, or person of God, shine on me was that I thought it would make me partake of its brightness, and I should thus be rendered different from other people, and I did not want thus to be; and I probably thought that it would be more pleasing to God for me to choose an humbler position, and so out of affected modesty refused it.

I kept my head covered the most if not all of the night, and passed a night of most horrible trouble. This was now the first trouble that I had experienced since my ll or profession. It is true I thought I had experiend trouble in those deep and mysterious revelations rough which I had been led. I was aware of their fficulty, but had Divine aid to help me through ; so twithstanding I had experienced some trouble I had it felt that anguish of soul that I experienced during e present night. It was truly a horrible wretched ght that I passed. Deep trouble may now be said to t in. I had, without knowing the direful consequences at it would bring on, disobeyed in three very imporut particulars. Had it have been impressed on me by od to have obeyed in either of these three last parculars, I think I should without doubt, have done . It though appeared to be left to my own choice, it had been throughout, which side to choose; d I here, as it happened, choose the wrong thing ch time. But had there been more difficulty attending ese last three things mentioned, I think I would ve been more apt to have obeyed, or choose the right de; for their performance I have no doubt would ave been comparatively easy to things I had been d through.' It was in those deep and difficult evelations and travels, that required all the energies f my soul; together with Divine aid, that I kept losest to the text. So when the plan for the univerl redemption of man was, as I believe, nearly com. leted it was spoilt (at least for the present) by my isobeying in these three things mentioned. Whether r not there remained much more to be done after accept- ig what was offered at either of these three times, I am ow unable to say ; but I am inclined to think that had I ave accepted, or done according to God's will in either f the three, that the business would soon have been nished, and the plan for the universal redemption of

man established; but all appeared to be lost by m
wanting something in my own way. We should take
things that are offered to us of God after His own will
and not after ours.

I expect the reader has been struck with wonder an
astonishment at the recital of the foregoing, and won
ders what it could all mean. I will say that I believe i
was the Millennium that was about to dawn, and that
if it had succeeded that the Gospel would soon have been
proclaimed with a saving effect to the uttermost bounds
of the earth, and the last man and woman have been
brought their Saviour to know. I believe it was the
Millennium about to dawn from the fact that I believe
those little children already mentioned, were moved to
sing that song on purpose for me, from the fact that it
took such an effect on me; and for other reasons which
have already been mentioned.

I now wish to go back and relate what I experienced
that I think has a refference or will have a bearing upon the present sectional troubles. At the close of one
of these lessons of revelation as I have called them, I
was greatly operated upon and arose and proclaimed to the family. I spake with great freedom, and
seemed like the words were put in my mouth as fast as
I could utter them. I proclaimed to them that myriads
and myriads of souls would be saved from endless per-
dition. At the time of which I now speak, I was moved with peculiar regard towards the African race.
Spencer, the boy that had lain across the door, was standing immediately to my left. I embraced him, putting
my left arm I believe, around his neck.

Seemed like I was to do something to greatly relieve
the condition of this race of people, but what it would
have been I am now unable to say, inasmuch as my

mission was not finished, but from what I experienced I am inclined to think that God is not satisfied with slavery as it now exists, and this cirumstance had been the foundation for my remarks on slavery. From what was afterwards made known to me, I am inclined to think that this related mostly to corporal punishments, and I have accordingly treated of it mostly in that light. This circumstance has certainly had the effect to cause me to look upon that race of people with peculiar regard ever since. This boy Spencer was a professor of religion, has since died, and I have no doubt is now at rest.

I will now return to the subject where I left off. It was now made known to me that the work could not be finished at this place, owing to the interruptions of the family, I mean their bothering me, their sinfullness, or something of the kind; but if I would go to my grandfather's, about six or seven miles distant, this work would there be renewed. Unfortunately I was prevented from doing this. My father no doubt thought that he could do the best by me and so refused to let me go. Divine influence appears mostly to have left me, and I was left to stem the torrent-in trouble and despair, so very grievous that I can't begin to describe it. As it is written, " no one hath power of himself to retain the Spirit." I had erred and He had taken His flight from me so far as these works were concerned, and I had no way to call Him back. My parents saw something was the matter, and various were the conjectures as to what it was. Some said that I had studied too hard; others that I was in love with some young lady; and some this thing, and some that. Unfortunately, the means taken for my recovery were entirely wrong, I was excluded from books, and, to a great extent, from society. This tended to throw me into deeper trouble. So great did my troubles eventually get to be, that I do not believe I slept a wink for many successive nights.— Throughout this trying time, I had as good health, I think, as I ever had in my life. I do not recollect being the least unwell, at any time. Nothing but Divine aid could thus have sustained me.

The intense trouble and distress that I suffered during these times can never be told.

About this time or probably sooner, I went down to the creek accompanied by one of my brothers and step brother. I had an irresistible desire to go in the water that the ordinance of baptism might be administered, but I was prevented much against my will. I made an attempt to go in the water at one other time but was prevented. My people kept such a close watch over me that I was not able to do in this matter as I wished. I was though still desirous that the ordinance of baptism should be administered, and thought if I could only get in the water that it was all I wanted—that I could then administer the ordinance myself. It was afterwards impressed on me that, under circumstances like mine, any mode that one has faith in will answer, be it sprinkling, pouring or what not. Notwithstanding, I believe Baptism to be an ordinance or a positive law; that there can therefore be but one mode, and that under ordinary circumstances we cannot obey or fulfill this ordinance only by doing just what is commanded. We saw that Moses could not obey at Kadesh in the desert of Zin, only by doing just what was commanded. Numerous other instances might be mentioned—such as Saul when he was sent to smite the Amelekites; institution of the Passover, &c., besides many others. I presume though enough has been mentioned to prove this point,

As it is written : "If ye love God ye will keep his commandments." I therefore believe that all true christians will have a desire to do respecting the mode of baptism just what they believe to be commanded of God. How carefully then we should study the Scriptures, casting aside all our prejudices and prepossessed opinions, in order that we may find out and follow the true mode!

I was desirous above all things of going to my grandfather's, in order that this work might be renewed, but was not permitted. My parents thought it was studying that ailed me, and so kept all books away from me. I was not even permitted to read the Bible itself. I had an insatiable desire for that book, and wished much to read it. Upon one occasion I, by some means, got hold of a testament and applied it to my bosom. Seemed like I was being possessed of its truths; there was a pleasant sensation springing up in my bosom, and I thought by holding the book thus that I would soon get a thorough knowledge of it without the trouble of studying, and likewise much sooner and more perfectly than I could otherwise have done.

There was a pleasant sensation springing up in my bosom, and I thought a knowledge of the Book would thus soon be imparted to me. At this juncture I was discovered by one of my brothers, and the Book forcibly torn away from me. Oh how badly it hurt me! Losing a fortune of millions would not have hurt me half so much. I was surely doing no one any harm there with the Book; and, had I eventually have found that I was not getting a knowledge of the Book in that way, I should have been certain to have taken it the slow but sure way—by reading. I have always regretted that I was not permitted to study the Scriptures about this time, because my appetite for them was so very keen, that I think I could have learned them much better than I fear I shall ever be able to do again.

Talking of worldly things was complete physic to me. My sole desire was to get back under the balmy influence of the Holy Ghost, and to a renewal of the work to which I had been called.

Because I could not see, do and believe as others did, I was considered deranged; and the report, I suppose, soon became general, that I was deranged from studying books or some other cause. That I did get into a species of mania I will admit, but it was only such as would result from taking up any sane, sound man and confining him. You may confine a well man, and it will assuredly make a mudman of him. I will illustrate this a little. There was once a maniac, or at least a person who was pronounced a fit subject for the lunatic asylum. Accordingly arrangements were made for his reception, and one of his friends started with him for that place. They soon reached the city and took lodging at a hotel. The next morning the supposed lunatic got up very early and took the paper of commitment out of his friend's pocket, and took a walk over to the asylum. Getting there he told the managers that after a little he would bring them a subject, and, says he, he will be certain to tell you that I am the one; but you must not mind that, but take him and take care of him, for that is only a way he has of doing. Our friend waking up and finding the lunatic gone, did not know what to think of it; but, he coming in soon afterwards, all was right again. After breakfast, he asked the lunatic if he would take a walk with him: he told him he would. They accordingly took a walk over to the asylum. As soon as they got there

the lunatic said to the managers that he had brought them that man, and running his hand in his pocket, pulled out and handed them the paper of commitment. They forthwith harnessed on to him, placed the straight jacket on him, and ushered him into a cell, he all the time hallooing as lustily as he could, that he was not the man; that the other man was the one. And had it not been that the relatives of the parties at home made known the true state of things, we do not know where the affair would have ended. My case was something similar to the above. After erring in those three important particulars I got into deep trouble. This though I think would have worn off after a little, had I been let alone. I think about this time I ate but little, or perhaps nothing for about a week; but notwithstanding this I did not feel the least inconvenience from it. My father talked of giving me medicine, thinking the condition of my system demanded it, but Oh how badly it sounded to me! I knew I was in the hands of one who doeth all things well. During this time I had not the least pain nor sickness that I know of, which, I doubt not, could not have been had I not been under Divine care. At length one day I got to playing with my fingures and hands on the head board of the bed where I was laying. It was on the same head board upon which that bright Image appeared to have sat. It appeared to make a pleasing or delightful sound to me, as it had been the Æolian harp. I was doing no one any harm that I know of, neither myself. I was doing this merely I suppose for pastime, and probably would soon have quit it of myself; but my father being solictious for my welfare had my hands tied down, as he afterwards told me, for fear that I would hurt them. This I believe was the first check that was put on my liberties. It soon exasperated me,

and caused me perhaps to say grievous things against the family. I had requested peaceably to go to my grand fathers where I had the promise of having these works renewed, but was not permitted to do so, as has already been stated, but instead thereof I was kept closely shut up in a room, and society to a great extent excluded. Even my little sisters that had sung the song "Millennium" so sweetly, and which I loved so well, (for I now loved them better than I ever had done before) and which I desired so much to be with me, were not permitted to come about me, as it was said by some of the family that they were afraid I would hurt them.

I was also desirous of going forth to spread the Gospel. My desire for this at one time in particular, was very great. I thought I could have conquered, or been the means or converting to Christianity, the whole earth in two full years. There were also other things of importance on my mind which I wished to get out to see about. With all these momentous things on my mind how could it be expected that I should do and act as I always had done? If it will make a man a maniac or a madman to confine him when he can see no cause for it, what was it calculated to do in my case? It hurt me seems like a hundred times worse if possible, to be pent up at that time than it would at any other time, and because I could not be calm and composed under these circumstances, and probably talked of things that the family knew nothing about I was considered beside myself. This may be compared to Festus' judgment of Paul upon a certain occasion when he pronounced him to be mad or beside himself.

I think there is no man, under the circumstances, after disobeying in these three important particulars, that

could have come out any better than I did, and I think the chances were 99 to 1 for any one similarly situated to have lost his life also. I don't think the trouble that Job suffered, although very grievous, would begin to compare with mine.

The circumstance of my brother taking the testament away from me, together with other things, at length caused me to believe that the family one and all were against me, and were for destroying the works that it was pleasing to God to call me to. A belief of this kind was sufficient to have broken the bonds between me and the dearest friend upon earth.

After I got to believe that the family was against me, and were for destroying these works I became strongly alienated from them, and the very persons that I a short time before had loved so well, that I would almost have died for, I now considered my enemies, and even spake grievous words against them. This caused me to be kept in closer confinement, as much I presume for their personal safety as any thing else.

But if I was an insane or mad man then I am now; for the things that I then believed I yet believe, and shall continue to do so as long as breath animates this body. The things that then took place as already described, are the plainest of any that have taken place during my life, and I never expect to forget them so long as I live, After being pent up some two months I was turned out as healed. In this time my enthusiasm for religion and nearly every thing else had died down, and I therefore consider that I was then in a worse condition than I had yet been in; but, inasmuch as the family thought I could be turned out with safety to themselves, I was liberated. But had I have obeyed in either of those three important particulars already

mentioned, I have no doubt but the designs of God would have been carried out, and would thus have been a saving of much trouble to myself, as well as to my parents and others, and would at the same time I trust, have been of some benefit to the human family. Or had I been permitted to have gone to my grand-fathers all I think, would still have been well. My father seeing there was something the matter with me, no doubt thought he could do a better part by me than would be done there, and without knowing the evil that he would thus inflict, refused to let me go. This was natural. I blame them though for guessing at the cause of my troubles, and treating me accordingly, when they were entirely mistaken. During all this time of intense trouble and mental suffering, I had the greatest love for the people of God. If my parents had got some christian person, one in whom I had confidence as a christian, to have conversed with me, the seat of my disease could soon have been discovered; but this was not done.

My reasons for writing thus much upon this latter part of my subject is, that as I was considered deranged, I wish my friends and others generally to know how it was, and have thus been particular in relating it; but it is yet very imperfect, I not having related near all that I might have done. My narrative from my call down to my profession of religion is tolerably perfect, or at least about as near so as I can relate it, with some four or five exceptions, three of which are very important; but I did not think proper to insert them in a work of this kind, and have therefore omitted them. My narrative from that time down to the close is still more imperfect, I not having related all that I might have done by a great deal. All taken together would fill a large

book, but I have endeavored to mention enough of the principal things so as to be understood. It is my intention some time or other, the Lord willing, to write out the whole. I will though for the present let the curtain fall over this part of my narrative.

CHAPTER XVI.

FURTHER ACCOUNT.

I now propose going back and mentioning a few things that I omitted.

I, at some time early in the work, or soon after my call, saw in a vision great cannon guns. I could see distinctly the wheels that they were mounted upon. Seemed like there was to be a great war, or great fighting some way. I though have never been able to tell exactly what this alluded to, or what it should mean. I presume I should have known all about it had my mission have been completed. If asked if I saw this by an eye of faith or with my natural eye, I would say by an eye of faith, though I saw them as plainly as if I had seen them with my natural eye.

The lightning and the two images of God, or God in person, if I may so speak, I saw with my natural eye as plainly as I ever saw the sun at noon-day.

AM TROUBLED IN A VISION.

I presume it was the third night after these works commenced on me, I saw a vision that troubled me much.

There was a man to be hung at Troy, Montgomery county, of the name of Nash, I believe. I seemed to

have been impressed on that I should go there to keep him from being hung, or at all events that he ought not to be hung. The night after he was hanged I saw this vision. Seemed like over to my right was wrapped in darkness, or at least it appeared of a shady or dark color. All of God's lights appeared to be put out except one small place which lay in the direction of the foot of the bed, but a little obliquely to the right. I could see devils on the wall to my right, dancing with infernal joy.

It appeared that all of God's lights were put out except that one small place which was represented by a golden color, and these devils appeared to be dancing over it for joy. I was in a great deal of trouble at seeing this you may be sure. I felt as if I was almost dead, and these devils were dancing for joy, probably at seeing God's lights so nearly put out and over my prostrate condition together. I was deeply involved in trouble but lay there and saw it all. How long it lasted or how it went away I now cant tell.

When I heard from the hanging which I believe was the next day, or at all events in a day or two, I heard that this young man protested his innocence to the last; and also that the first time they swung him off the rope broke. They then tied him up again and the next time succeeded in hanging him. I was not surprised to hear of the rope breaking, but I was sorry to hear that they tied him up again and at last succeeded in hanging him. I thought as the rope had broken the first time that he ought then to have been let off. Though I believe he was generally believed to have been guilty of the crime for which he was hanged, I yet believe there is something wrong about it.

C B

ANOTHER VISION.

The one that I am now a going to give an account of I dont know that I can hardly call it a vision, because I saw it in the day time and with my natural eye as plainly as I ever saw any thing. But without being particular as to the name I will relate what I saw. I was laying on a bed in the room one evening probably about the middle of the afternoon or perhaps later, and I saw immediately on the wall in front of me a picture as of a good stout boy. The personage was that of a fat baby without clothing and in the attitude of running north—the direction of the wall. The color was a vivid red, though a deeper red than red hot iron; on his head there was something like a breadtray; upon the top of that there was a wild goose; and on the top of that there was a bull's head having horns; all appeared to be of the same vivid red color. Immediately to the right of this was a ball about the size of a half dollar, or perhaps near that of a dollar, with a streak running upward for two or three feet, of about the size of a pipe stem. This was likewise of that same vivid red color. I saw all this with perfect composure, not being scared nor troubled in the least that I recollect of. After remaining there for sometime, probably a half hour, perhaps longer, it began to fade away. The image of the little boy faded away first, then the tray or what ever it was, and so on. The last thing that disappeared was the bull's head and horns. Whether this ball and streak upward faded away at the same time I do not now recollect, but I presume they did. What this that I have described, could mean I can't fully tell, for the object of all was not made known to me. The bread tray, wild goose and bull's head were for emblems which I deem unnecessary to mention here. The balance I dont know what they were for unless they were to add force and character to these three as emblems. It was represented to me that, had this streak from the ball have extended downward instead of upward, that instant combustion would have taken place. I will state here that there was a sign of this streak on the wall for years afterwards. It left a whitish stain and was there a year or two ago.

A REVELATION.

I will give the reader an account of a revelation, or what I experienced in one of those lessons as I have been calling them. I was laying in the room on a bed (the same room where I had seen all those visions, &c., with the exception of those of the first night,) and there came over a gentleman to see me. He sat and talked with my father in a passage near where I was laying. Whilst laying here I commenced reflecting on a circumstance that had occurred between this gentleman and myself. He had once told a falsehood and proved himself right by another person, which did not help the matter much. I was loser by this to a small amount. After awhile my father came in the room where I was, and said that such a gentleman, naming him, had come and wished to see me. I told him that I did not wish to see him at that time, and requested that he should not come in the room where I was, and also I believe requested that no one else should come in to disturb me. In the meantime, God I believe had commenced making known to me some things concerning this matter between this gentleman and myself, and that was the reason that I did not wish to be disturbed. And in order that I might not be disturbed by this gentleman nor my father coming in the room, I got up and proped the door after him. As I lay on the bed I fell into a trance and God began to make known to me some things relative to this matter. I thought this gentleman was to suffer death for thus telling a lie, and I thought I heard a knife being made in the shop as plainly as I ever heard any thing in my life, with which to cut his throat. Notwithstanding I had requested my father not to come in the room, he came and pushed open the door and came in, remarking that he could open the door. If it had been this other gentleman, that had come in after I had requested that he should stay out, I was to have gotten up and moved my right hand down obliquely across him at which he was to have fallen down dead as did Ananias. But I did not want him to come in the room, and so after my father went out I got up and shut the door, and proped it again. It was, seem like with the utmost difficulty that I could shake off this spell enough to get up, but I made out to do so and proped the door good this time, and then went and lay down again. Soon after laying down the chair with which the door was proped commenced cracking, like it was strained. It was made known to me that God could open the door though it was proped, and it appeared that if I had not believed this, that the chair would instantly have been broken in pieces and the door opened, but I believed and the cracking ceased. I believe I told you about hearing the hammer going to make the knife with which to kill this gentleman. I could hear the hammer in the distance as plainly as I ever heard it in a shop in my life, and it appeared that this gentleman's throat was to be cut and he pitched into outer darkness. Although it was represented to me that he should have been put to death, it was now by a deep and mysterious revelation made appear to me that he should not be put to death, and so the matter ended.

I am not able fully to tell the meaning of the foregoing revelation, and I do not know that it is necessary for me to know. I presume it had the desired effect on me, let it have been what it may.

This gentleman was a professor of religion, and was also in the church; and it was probably from that circumstance that his crime was represented to me as being so wicked as to be worthy of death.

This revelation being upon a separate subject I have been able to give it entire, or at least as much so as I am able. I though can't begin to express it in words just as it was, or as it appeared to me. The balance of the revelations that I experienced were mostly upon one subject, or one continuous subject as it were, and are therefore mixed and blended together in such a way that I am not able to give any of them entire and separate. The foregoing is the only one that I can give a separate account of.

CHAPTER XVII.

GENERAL REVIEW.

Well my friends you have heard my story all through.

Now to prove that the foregoing is no fabrication of my own, I will mention the following incidents.

In the first place I will here remark that I have related these things in the main as herein set forth, to probably an hundred persons from the date of their occurrence down to the present time. To some I have related one part, and to others, another, but at the same time I don't suppose that any thing that I have thus related to my friends will conflict with any thing that is herein set forth.

And to prove farther that the effect of what I then experienced has been on me for some time, and that I have been trying to get a part at least, of these things accomplished, I refer to the following.

Some four years ago, Dr. John Shaw and Col. Wm. B. Richardson were candidates for the General Assembly. The subject of slavery or treatment of servants, having been on my mind for a great while, and as yet nothing done towards providing for their better treatment, and which I thought should be done, I set down and wrote each of these gentlemen a letter stating some certain laws that I was desirous of seeing passed, and among them was that relative to slavery which in the main, I believe, was put down as herein set forth. I desired an answer from each, intending to vote for the one that came nearest my views. As it was but a short time before the election, it so turned out that I did not get an answer from either of the gentlemen, and so I did not vote for either.

And further, at the next sitting of the last Legislature, when Messrs W. D. Dowd and Alex. Kelly were members from Moore, I wrote to them concerning the same subject, and among other laws that I was desirous of seeing passed was that for the better treatment of servants, in the main as herein set forth.

These gentlemen, though concurring in at least a portion of my views, said there was such a press of other business, and my letter too coming somewhat late in the session, that they could not attend to it. So with these remarks I hope the reader will at least conclude that I have been conscientious in saying what I have upon the subject of slavery.

But it may be argued that as I had got into such a troubled state of mind, as has already been described, that I may be conscientious in relating what I have and at the same time be mistaken. In answer to this I will here state that the most of the things that I experienced and have herein set forth, took place before I got into that distressed state of mind and I therefore think there is no just ground for that belief. It is true I experienced some deep trouble whilst being led in those deep and mysterious waters, and being submitted to trial as it were, to prove whether or not I was suitable for the arduous undertaking. But at length I was lead to a clear sunshine as it were, where there appeared to be no difficulties, and I there erred in the discharge of duties the performance of which, I have no doubt, would have been comparatively easy to some that I had been brought through, as has been before stated. It was then that deep and unutterable trouble set in. The trouble that I experienced previous to that time, though at some few times, very great, yet was not so distressing, from the fact that Divine aid was with me and I was soon helped over them. Although the latter part was truly a distressing time to me, yet, God has blessed me with a perfect retention of memory, and I recollect all the important things that took place throughout, as well as many or most, of the smaller.

Again my professing religion in about twelve hours after my call may, I think, be considered some evidence that I was called in a miraculous manner and intended for a special purpose. My profession was attended with power, such that I have not been able to doubt for a moment since, of its perfect genuineness; though I have sined and done many things not right since.

That I must have been called and for a special purpose, I think is evident from the following:

Unless I had been called of God for a special purpose I think it appears singular that I should have been called apparently in favor with God within a few moments or minutes after my call, and also that I should thus have been called, and have had the wonderful works of God placed on me while I was yet in my sins as it were. Though as I have elsewhere remarked, I felt the burden and weight of sin which I believe began gradually to be removed, and from that time until I professed I felt easy and contented as to a future state. But I had not as yet experienced that outpouring of the spirit, and felt that inexpressible joy such as the convert feels; but still I had experienced a very great change, such probably as I should have taken for religion had I experienced no greater change, as has been elsewhere stated.

And further, when I came from Carthage there was nothing of the kind that I know of upon me. I acted pretty much as I always had done, only I may perhaps have been more cheerful than usual, owing to causes already mentioned. I will here remark that I talked of going that night with the boys a fishing, but my father wished me to remain with him, and I did so. I will also remark that I had never been a serious seeker of religion. I had never so much as been in an altar to be prayed for, though I had been impressed on that it was my duty to go, but I had never, that I know of, been very seriously impressed upon the subject of religion. It is true I sometimes had had some impressions, but they had generally worn off without leaving any very serious effect. I will mention one of these. Probably some three or four years previous to the time of which I am now speaking, I was at a neighbor's at a corn shucking. We had finished the corn and had gone down to the house, and I think had also eaten supper. At all events the most of the company were standing in the hall part of the house. It was about the time that Miller, the supposed prophet, had predicted that the world was to be at an end, the conversation turned upon this subject. At length the gentleman of the house started to get one of Miller's pamphlets, describing this prediction. About this time I began seriously to reflect on my case, knowing that I would certainly be lost were this thing to come as predicted, and find me in my present condition. The consequence was I soon began to feel sick, and the first thing I knew I was down on the floor, and several persons around shaking me; I had fainted. This though, I believe soon wore off without leaving any very lasting impression.

I was what the world might call a moralist, and though a great sinner, there were some sins, such as cursing, swearing, &c., that I was a stranger to.

It is also, I think, evident that the works that I experienced were not necessary for the salvation of one soul alone; and it is also evident that what I experienced was out of the line of common experience, or such as people commonly experience in the profession of religion. Hence I think it is fair to conclude that as I had experienced more than common that the e was also something more than common intended by it.

It was told me why it was that I had experienced more than was common—such as seeing the lightning, image or person of God, hearing those sounds, deep revelations, &c. It was to endue me with strong faith, it being represented to me that I had a difficult road to pass through, and that it was necessary that my faith should thus be strong in order that I might hold out to the end of the journey. As I have elsewhere said, there was nothing of a compulsory nature used towards me in this work, but all appeared to be left to my own choice; therefore unless my faith had been strong, I should have been more apt to have deviated from the path of duty. And though my faith was as strong seem like as it could well be, it appeared to be with the greatest difficulty that the work could be accomplished. My faith or regard for these works at that time was so great that I believe I would have died before I would have surrendered them. I will here remark that the difficulty, &c., of the road was kept concealed, and I only knew that it was difficult by passing over it, or after I had passed over it, it was then that the object of my having been so greatly wrought upon was made known to me, and not before I commenced the journey.

It was also at some time during the work made known to me that no one, since the days of Christ and the Apostles, had experienced such works as I had, and unless they have in a little over fourteen years, I don't suppose they yet have.

I will state here that I attribute my professing religion so early as the twelve hours from the beginng of my call, to the family disturbing me, and bearimg me to bed, as has been before described. Whether or not I should otherwise have professed so soon, I am unable to say. I was at that time under Divine influence and had a pleasant sensation upon me, such as I can't describe.

As I have elsewhere remarked that, that calmness and serenity of disposition that I experienced, I should probably have taken for religion had I experienced no greater change, for sin had not appeared to be in my way from the time that I felt its burden, as a weight on my breast removed. This burden remained but a short time and did not trouble me much from the fact that I was soon helped over it.

Strange as it may seem I shed not a tear nor made a moan for my sins that I know of from the time of my call to profession of religion. And when I had a vision of that horrible place, hell, I had not the least fears i or apprehensions so far as my own personal safety was concerned.

And again to prove that this could not possibly have been a mental delusion I refer to my profession of religion, and in so short a space of time from the time of beginning; for who ever heard of a single instance of any one under mental delusion professing religion, and in the short space of time too of twelve hours from the time of commencement thereof. Is not this circumstance enough to prove that my case was an extraordinary one, and that I was operated upon with unusual power.

And farther if I was under mental delusion how is it that I have a perfect retention of memory throughout. Many of these things that I recollect and have herein set forth are also recollected by the members of the family; we do not differ as to our belief concerning these things, but recollected them in the main precisely alike. As we recollect these things alike, why will not my judgment do to depend on concerning things that they have forgotten, or such as they never knew? And farther, to prove that this was a work of God that was upon me I will mention some important truths that were made known to me at some time during my travel.

It was made known to me that the reason that we can use our right hand better than our left is, that God will save his elect on his right hand, we having this visble sign in our bodies to teach us that such will certainly be the case. As the rainbow is a sign that the earth will not again be destroyed by water, so is this a sign that God will save his elect on his right hand. The circumstance of the rainbow was not made known in connection therewith, but is merely a comparison of my own. Another:

I was greatly operated upon respecting the Roman Catholic church, and from what I experienced I have indubitable reasons for believing that that church, as it now exists, is not acceptible to God. Another:

I at some time during my travel, but now can't tell the exact time, became impressed with the idea that I could impart the Holy Ghost by laying on of hands; and al o that by standing in front of a person and putting the inside tips of my thumbs and fingures to the corresponding ones of the other person, that I could have imparted other important gifts. I will here remark that at that time I don't think I was well enough to read in the scriptures to recollect that the Apostles had, by laying on of hands, imparted the Holy Ghost.

I will mention one other.

I became impressed, perhaps by revelation, that every man, woman and child is possessed with the inate principle of God and devil, so as to answer in the same place of a personal God and devil. For instance, if you pray to God the spirit of God that is in you hears and answers this prayer the same as if God in person were to attend to it, and that you can thus seek and obtain religion the same as if God were personally to attend to you. Resist the devil and he will flee from you. Be ye therefore perfect even as your Father which is in heaven is perfect. You can thus, I think, practice the works of God and grow in grace until this wicked spirit will become almost, or quite, extinct.

But on the other hand, if you cultivate the evil spirit, and neglect the good Spirit, you will grow in wickedness, and it will eventually choke or destroy the good Spirit. Then will be fulfilled that which is written "My spirit shall not always strive with man." The Spirit of God will take its everlasting flight, and that man or that woman be given up to a state of eternal reprobation. To make my position plainer I will state that I believe there to be as many Gods and devils as there are human beings, each man and each woman possessing this inate principle of God and devil as aforesaid.

And I further believe that a personal God or a personal devil has but very little to do with the salvation of man in the one case, or his destruction in the other. I will illustrate this a little. We will say that a man makes a machine for the performance of any work whatever. It is made after his own model and fashions the work according to his own will. So I compare the plan of salvation upon man, or for man to a machine that is continually going, and will shape Godliness if the person for whom it is operating is willing or desirous that such should be the case, and will come within prescribed limits. But at the same time if they do not obey the promptings of the Spirit, and will not come within prescribed limits, it will shape their destruction or ruin; it shapes Godliness or ruin, heaven or hell so to speak, according to the will of the person for whom it is operating.

God is desirous that it should shape Godliness or Salvation for all, and impresses on them all to that effect; but at the same time it will shape ruin should the person for whom it is operating desire such, or even neglect to do his part. I will remind all that I believe this machine as is now running is shaping for every man and woman in the land salvation or destruction—heaven or hell as it were. How important it is then that we attend to it and have it to shape for us, the thing we so much need. This plan of Salvation, or machine as I compare it to, is always and eternally going the same; so that one can get religion at any time and any place as well as another. Wherever you go this Spirit of God is still with you, and oftentimes striving to win you over. Although God is represented as being omnipotent and omniscient, I think it would be quite a task for him to attend personally to all the little things of this world. I will remark here that according to the plan mentioned, I believe it is worked according to his will as though He were personally to attend to all these things; it is only a way He has to work his will so to speak. A machine that does work according to the will of the owner, does not always require his presence in order to do the work: so I think with the plan of salvation. I will here remark that I do not believe that the two Spirits, good and evil, can exist in union in man; and that they are therefore constantly battling for the ascendancy, and that eventually one or the other will predominate to the utter exclusion of the other.

I think I have reasons for the believing as I do upon this subject, and unless I had believed it, I should not have put it forth.

Before closing this part of my subject I wish to make a few remarks upon a subject that I have not treated upon as fully as I wished.

The reader has doubtless noticed, at different times and places through the book, where it is mentioned, "things were revealed to me," "things were made known to me," &c. These terms are very nearly allied to each other. Perhaps you may wish to know how they were revealed or made known to me, as the case may be. When things of importance, and where they required much length of time, were being revealed to me, I was in a kind of a trance as has been elsewhere stated; and I presume pretty much insensible to all objects except the one in which I was immediately concerned. At such times I don't suppose I moved a hand or a foot in the time, but lay perfectly still. When things were revealed to me or my mind enlightened on any particular, there was no audible voice used. It appeared to flow into my breast creating a perceptible but not an unpleasant sensation. Though there was no voice used I thought it was the plainest talking that I had ever experienced. I don't recollect hearing any sounds of a supernatural kind after the first night of my call, except the cracking of the chair, hammer in the distance, rapping at the door, and some others that I heard upon one other occasion, but which I will not mention here, inasmuch as I have not mentioned the incident connected therewith. These lessons or revelations as I have called them, would last probably half an hour, or probably as long as an hour, whether longer or shorter I can't tell. I only know that they were sometimes of pretty smart duration. But I think I have many times been enlightened upon subjects when I was not in trance as it were. These, though I think, were always of short duration. I mean they were not long in being made known to me.

With these remarks I leave this part of the subject with the reader.

CHAPTER XVIII.

CONCLUSION.

We now come to take our last view of the matter, and in doing so I wish once more to urge upon you, my countrymen, the great dangers by which we are now surrounded as a nation and people, and the great importance of putting a stop to this war in some way—by going back into the Union if it can't be done in any other way. I know this will sound badly to a great many persons, but the two evils, going back into the Union, or risking the chance of fighting through, are now upon us, and one or the other of these two things will eventually have to be done before these difficulties can be settled. It is now too late to take steps to avoid these difficulties. If our public men could now be back at the starting point of these difficulties, with the experience that they now have, they would, I think take more pains to avoid this war, but it is now too late. The war is upon us, and certain it is that we can't long exist as a nation, neither the North nor the South, in a war carried on upon such a gigantic scale as the present one is.

With the terrible blow that has already been stricken, and with the prospect of future difficulties ahead, I think it a deplorable case whether we succeed in building up this Southern Confederacy, or whether we eventually have to go back into the old Union: in either case both sections of the country will be clad in mourning for many days to come. I think of the two evils, we should choose the less, and try and put an end to this terrible civil war—this great and bloody struggle.

For the war threatens soon to rage with more fury

than ever, and our young men of both sections will probably soon be cut down and scattered to and fro like leaves driven by the Autumn wind.

We have a terrible foe of more than two to one to contend against, besides a large floating population—I mean emigrants coming from Europe and other countries; we have none. They also have a large and powerful navy; we as good as none. They also have in their possession and cut off from us together some of our most fertile lands. And if under these circumstances we conquer, the God of battles, I think, must certainly be with us.

As I said before it will be a bad case should we eventually have to go back in the old union, and it is I think also a bad chance to risk the chance of fighting through with this great odds against us. I think under the circumstances it becometh us as a philanthropic people, to choose of the two evils the one that we consider best for the present and rising generations, for time and for eternity. I think under the circumstances, we had best put a stop to this war for the present by going back into the Union; and should time demonstrate that we can't live well together, let us separate by compromise; there is no need of having fighting about it. We have territory enough for two great and powerful countries, if our people would divide and settle it up, instead of killing up each other in cruel wars. I will take occasion to remark here that if our tariff and system of trade to the North and to Europe had continued the same, that I believe much would have been gained to the South by peaceable secession. But at the same time, I believe by passing laws, some such as has already been mentioned, and to a certain extent adopting a non intercourse with the North, and doing our trade direct to Europe, that all the advantages of secession might have been secured to us, and we yet have remained in the Union, and at the same time have created no unfriendly feeling towards the Northern people, or at all events no unfriendly feeling of a serious nature. As I have said elsewhere, I was for passing these laws not as a retaliatory step towards the Northern people for what they have done, but I think it was actually necessary for our well being as a people. The North had been getting too much of our substance, and I think there should have been some way devised to put a stop to it.

I will here remark again, that under the circumstances, I think it best to put a stop to this war by going back into the Union as aforesaid, for the following reasons. In the first place, you will please permit me to say again, that I do not believe the causes were justifiable of secession. In the second place, I do not think secession was properly conducted; if we chose to secede, I think we should have done so by the popular vote. In the third place, I do not think the institution of slavery as it now exists, will do to risk a revolution upon. I say this notwithstanding I am the owner of servants myself. And in the fourth and last place, I do not believe we can accomplish what we have undertaken to do. I therefore think we had best go back into the Union, and go soon, for I see no use in holding out, and having a great many of our young men killed up, and then eventually have to go back. I have been candid and sincere in speaking upon this subject as I have, and if I have said any thing not agreeable to the reader, I will inform him that it is the solemn dictates of my bosom, founded upon things already mentioned, together with a desire of soon seeing the evils of war removed from our once happy country, that has prompted me thus to speak. So my friends let us try the North once more. Let us see if this great party, the democratic party at the North, will do what they say they will do. And should we eventually wish to get off, I have not a doubt but we can do so better at some future time, and at a less sacrifice, both of life and property, than we can at present.

It will be discovered that I have advised going back into the Union as the surest and best mode of putting a stop to this wicked war. My arguments for this have already been mainly set forth. It is evident that we can't long exist as a nation, neither the North nor the South if we thus keep on. I presume you have heard the story of the Kilkenny cats, but in order to make sure of it, I will relate it. It is said that a gentleman once caught a couple of these cats, and after tying their tails together, threw them across a pole. They commenced fighting and fought on until it is said, there was only one and a half inches of their tails left. So why must we, the people of the North and the South verify this story upon ourselves? Why must we wear each other out before striking for a peace. These same difficulties will at last be to settle. I presume we all would like to see how this matter will terminate, but the way things are now going on, I presume many of us will first have gone to that home from whence no traveler returns.— It seems evident that we can never achieve our liberties, and get back our territory now in possession of the enemy, by force of arms, only by an awful sacrifice of life and property, even if we do then; and disastrous indeed will be the result should we persist in making this mighty effort and then eventually be crushed in it. By going back in the Union both sections will lay down their arms, and the territory that has been conquered from us, and now in possession of the enemy, will no doubt be restored to us. Then in a few years, if things do not work together well, we can try this thing again and come out in a body and likewise bring with us the balance of our territory now in possession of the enemy. Should time demonstrate that the two sections can't live together in union so as to be of mutual advantage to each other, I think it would be bad policy in either section to desire a further union. But let each side now lay down their arms, quit pushing against each other, and in my opinion the war will cease almost instantly. One side is pushing because the other is pushing, and neither side I presume can hardly tell what they are pushing about.

Again the North now has much of the fairest portion of our country in their possession—that portion that could be most depended on to support a war. These fair portions are not only cut off from us, but the soldiers from these portions, and likewise many refugees from the same section, are now among us, and have to be sustained by the thinner and less grain-growing sections. In case of short crops and from other causes, our people have in times of peace depended much on the eastern part of the State for grain and other useful commodities. How will we do now when this section instead of being an advantage to us, is actually a disadvantage so far as provisions are concerned. And upon top of this the major part of our working class is now in the army; so there are but comparatively few left behind to raise the necessaries of life. And farther, it takes a great deal more to do soldiers in an army than it would the same people at home. So if things thus keep on, have we not a prospect ahead of a famine—a very grievous famine, such as has not yet been in all the land, and that before a great while? Shall we wait until these things come quite to our door before making any arrangements to meet them? Shall we, like Mexico, (in the war with the United States) wait for the enemy to fight quite through and conquer the whole of our country before striking for a peace, or endeavoring to bring about a reconciliation between the two sections? So under these circumstances I think we had best back down and go back in the Union again, humiliating as it may appear. And should we find it necessary to try secession again, I think we should first go to work and make necessary preparations, such as erecting the necessary manufacturies among us, importing largely of the necessaries of life, such as we can't raise, so that we might live free and independent of other nations in a coming strife, should we have one.

The effects of this war will be felt bad enough to wind it up now without carrying it any farther. One having a leg or an arm broken, for instance, suffers more with it three or four days after it is done than right at the time of the accident. So of this war. I think we will feel the effects of it more a year or two hence than we do now.

From what I experienced above fourteen years ago I have no more doubt but what God was dissatisfied with slavery as it then existed than I have of my own existence. Whether or not he intends its final overthrow remains yet to be told. I was though principally impressed towards them as regards to better treatment. And inasmuch as my mission was not completed I am unable to say positively what disposition was intended to be made of them. Taking every thing into consideration, and for reasons already given, I am inclined to think that we had best keep them as they are, or at least until we get more light upon the subject. I am though well aware that this is no time to agitate the slavery question; so I think we had best attend to the condition of our country first and try and stop this cruel war and bring about a peace between the two sections and then attend to the servants afterwards.

Taking all these things in consideration, together with the great haste with which the South acted, that resulted first in secession, and from that to the war, I am inclined to think that the Southern Confederacy cant long stand upon its present foundation. My heart is filled with sadness when I reflect upon the condition of our once happy country. These things that I have stated are my solemn convictions and while it is no pleasure for me to speak as I have at many places done, I do so truly hoping that the worst may yet be averted from our once happy country. I will state here that I have been looking for something of the kind ever since those important truths were made known to me. It may be asked me if I were in possession of such knowledge as this why I did not make it known sooner, or try and do something to avert the coming difficulties.

One reason that I have not before given my experience to the world is that I have been constantly looking forward, hoping that God would call me to this great work again. And as regards doing something to try and avert the coming troubles I will state that I wrote some pieces which I hoped at least would have had some effect in avoiding a civil war, but I could not get them published, from the fact I presume, that they savored too strongly of Union sentiments. I did what I could to avert a civil war notwithstanding I somewhat thought there was a Divine object to be

accomplished by it; and if so, that I would be wrong
in saying or doing anything that would stop it, even if
I could, though half the nation were to get killed in it.
Notwithstanding this my philanthropic desires for my
fellowman were such that I was for using my influence
if I had any for stopping this dreadful calamity. And I
would have used still greater exertions had there been
any prospect of doing any good thereby; but seeing that
I could not effect anything, I with sorrow shrank back,
feeling almost certain that there was immense trouble
ahead.

It seems that one might about as well have commanded the Maelstrom to stand still, or have attempted to dam up the waters of the mightly Mississippi as
to have tried to stop the secessionists in their mad career·
They rushed on from union to secession, from that to
war, and from that to ultimate ruin I may say, if this
war be not speedily closed, with a heedlessness that knew
no bounds. Now that they have learned a lesson by practical experience, they will probably be more cautious in
the future.

Before closing this chapter I wish if possible to impress on the reader that I am sincere and candid in
writing what I have; that I have no desire to deviate
from truth, neither to the right nor the left if I know it,
and that I wish to speak nothing but what is really
true.

To prove that I had some idea of this war (either a
correct or an incorrect one) I refer the reader to the
following incident.

About the time the first volunteers were getting up,
and volunteering was popular, one of my friends and
relatives of Carthage was urging on me to volunteer. I
merely remarked to him that if every body knew what

I did, there would not be a volunteer in the State, (this I am able to prove.) I promised him at some time or other, I would give him my reasons for so speaking; I have not yet done so, but if I had, they would have been in the main, pretty much the same as is herein set forth.

And further, to prove that these works (not relative to the war) has been on me a good while, I refer to the following.

I was in Norfolk, Virginia, in the summer of 1855, during that dreadful scourge of yellow fever. I yet believing that God had some purpose in letting me live, was not afraid in the least of taking the fever, and so visited the sick and went about the streets whithersoever my business called me, not feeling scared in the least.

About this time as I was returning one evening to my boarding house, I met one of the boarders coming out of the house, who said to me that Warren was very sick, and of yellow fever as he supposed. Says he we are leaving and I advise you to do the same. I was though determined that the young man should not lay there and die neglected in that way though it might be yellow fever he had, and so I went up into his room and conversed with him and soon became satisfied that it was not the yellow fever he had. I went down and told the lady of the house that such a one of the boarders was sick, what I thought was the matter with him and what I thought would relieve him if she would have it done. She thinking it must be yellow fever and sent off immediaty for a doctor; he soon came, went up and examined the young man and pronounced it colic. He not having the necessary medcine with him, asked me if I would go down to the drugstore and get it for him; I told him I would, I went and got the medicine, he gave it to him and the young man was soon well. Warren told me afterwards that, had it not been for me he thought, he should have died as he could not have stood it long in that condition.

There was another one of my acquaintances in town very sick. I went in to see him. As soon as I went in he held out his hand to me, but he was speechless. I took him by the hand and remained with him a short time. He died soon after I left the room.

I came very near remaining and being of all the service that I could to the sick. At that time as the number of new cases was fast decreasing it was thought that the Fever would soon die out. Under these circumstances, I, being on expenses, and out of employment, concluded to leave the city. I went about eighty miles into the country and there took up for the time. Soon after leaving, the fever broke out with increased violence; O how my heart yearned for these people! It was the works that I had experienced in the spring of 1848 that caused me thus to be fearless in the midst of the yellow Fever. Therefore I had no fears of being taken with sicknes unto death, and never had better health than during my sojourn among the Fever. So if I risk my life I wish it to be in doing good to my fellow man, like Howard the good, and not in cruel and wicked wars.

Before closing, perhaps the reader may wish to know a little of my own case. I will state that I have never yet joined any church; and what is a great deal worse I have backsliden and sined in the sight of heaven and against Divine light. I think it is owing to some of these sins, together with againgt remisness of duty, that the work has never been renewed. I will here remark that there is a very important thing connected with this work that I have totally neglected. It has not been treated on in this work from the fact that I first want more light upon it before making it public. It is one of those four or five things omitted, that was made known to me during the first night of my call. It is of such a nature that I shall first probably have to go to Europe or Asia and then perhaps learn a language before it can be accomplished. This work is of an inseperable nature as it were, and is such that it seems that the balance that I experienced cant avail much without it and though it was fourteen years the 28th of last March since my call I have done nothing with it yet, and so far as I know this business remains as it was the first night of my call.

I have resolved though as soon as circumstances will permit to take some preparatory steps towards accomplishing this thing, but then, if the spirit of God be not placed on me it will all avail nothing.

To prove that I have been under the influence of God, and that it is that influence that has caused me to write the present work, I will mention one other incident.

Some six or eight months, or perhaps longer, I can't tell the exact time, after my call, I wrote off a history of my experience, &c., pretty much as is herein set forth, and have it now in manuscript, but in writing the present, I wished to be a little more particular in giving the details, and so in writing this I never so much as once looked at my old manuscript.

These things are now about as plain in my mind as the day they happened. Nothing else I think but the power of God could have impressed them so indelibly upon me.

I will state here that at the time of my call and previous thereto, I enjoyed universal cheerfulness and saw, I presume, as much pleasure as a most any young man a going. But since that time my heart has been sad, and I have suffered much remorse of conscience in consequence of the failure of this work, and many a bitter moment have I spent concerning it both by day and by night.

Queen Elizabeth, of England, when on her death bed is said to have exclaimed "millions and milli[ons] for one inch of time." So would I give milli[ons] millions if I had them, if I could only be back [at] of those places where I erred. Ah! worlds itself [is] nothing in comparison, and I would freely giv[e if] I had them, were I back at one of these place[s I] erred, that I might shape my course of anew.

I will now soon conclude, and before doi[ng so I] wish to say one more word to you, my country[men. I] have endeavored to set forth in an impartial v[iew the] cause of our sectional troubles, and I have also [endeav]ored to show that if we are in an error, we n[eed not] expect heaven to crown our efforts.

I have also given it as my opinion, that un[der the] circumstances it would be best for us to thro[w down] our arms and go immediately back into the U[nion. I] have already given my arguments concerning t[he mat]ter, and now my friends, I submit it to you[r own] judgment for you to decide as you may think b[est.]

I may have said many things in the foregoi[ng trea]tise not pleasing to my readers, but they will [I hope] pardon me for so saying, when I inform them th[at all] I have said upon this subject, has been with a desire of discharging a duty that I think I owe to my God and fellow man, and that I have desired to speak nothing but what I believed to be strictly true.

[Sidebar:] laid down on page 93, which, I doubt not, can now be easily done, if we will strike for this while victory rests upon our arms. In case this or its equivalent be not granted us, I see no chance but to fight through to the bitter end.

Seems like I can't well end this important subject without once more repeating that I desire soon to see peace and contentment reign throughout the entire length and breadth of our land, and that it may soon blossom and teem with happiness and the blessing of God, as the rose. Yea, that our sectional troubles may soon be settled peaceably, honorably and fairly, that peace and good will may soon reign throughout our entire land, and that the shadow of the most high God may rest upon us as a nation and people, and upon the whole world, is the sincere desire of one who wishes you well.

THE END.

APPENDIX.

(1.) It is said that only 10,000 votes were cast for members to the State Convention that passed South Carolina out of the Union; 10,000 out of 60,000. It is easy to see why the secessionists were unwilling to ratify or reject the ordinance at the polls.—*Semi-Weekly Observer, January* 28*th*, 1861.

Note.—The date at the bottom of the following references shows the date of the Fayetteville Semi-Weekly Observer, in which these references may be found, unless otherwise mentioned. The date may also be understood to be 1861, unless otherwise mentioned.

(2.) An Act passed by the General Assembly concerning the Convention that was voted for on the 28th of February, 1861—

SECTION 10. Be it further enacted, That no ordinance of this Convention shall have any force or validity until it shall have been ratified by a majority of the qualified voters for members of the General Assembly, to whom it shall be submitted according to the mode prescribed for elections of members to the House of Commons, the assent or dissent of the people hereto being expressed, as in preceding sections of this act.—*Feb.* 4.

(3) WASHINGTON, April 8th.

THE SOUTHERN COMMISSIONERS NOT RECOGNIZED BY THE SECRETARY OF STATE.

The state department replied to-day to the note of the commissioners from the Confederate States, declining to receive them in an official capacity, but expressing deference for them as gentlemen.—*Obr. file.*

(4.) If the correspondent of the New York Herald is to be believed, there is doubtless a force off Charleston ere this, and the change of policy which leads to this is the refusal of General Beauregard to allow of an evacuation of Fort Sumter, and a demand of the humiliation of a regular surrender, as of an army in an actual state of war.

If this this be so, it is plain that the Confederate States will not allow of peace. And the world will hold them responsible for the horrible civil war which will result. All that they ought to expect of a great and proud people is the simple evacuation of the fort. This is all that their necessities or their national honor requires. And in demanding humiliation and dishonor they go a step beyond the most extreme feeling of conciliation.—*April 11th.*

(5.) We hear that it is stated on all hands, even in Charleston, that the only thing in the way of the evacuation of Fort Sumter, was the requirement that its garrison should surrender as prisoners of war—a monstrous demand from those who profess to seek peace, as a condition precedent to the departure of the troops of a government at peace with them, from a fort belonging to that government.—*April 15th.*

(6.) General Beauregard refused to receive the fort as a surrender to South Carolina, but that it must be given up to the Southern Confederacy and the officers surrender themselves as prisoners of war, otherwise he will take the fort.—*April 8th.*

(7.) When the government determined to order Maj. Anderson out of the fort, it was on the condition that the property in it should not be molested but allowed to remain as it was. The authorities of the Confederate States would not agree to this, but manifested a disposition to get possession of the fort and the property therein. The government would not submit to such humiliation, and it was immediately determined to keep Maj. Anderson in the fort.—*Observer file. Date not recollected.*

(8.) It is believed that Maj. Anderson was ordered to leave with the remainder of his command in the usual way of detailing officers and men to different posts, but Gen. Beauregard was not willing to have a government steamer come into Charleston harbor and take away his enemy. He wanted a surrender of the fort.—*April 15th.*

(9.) The ball opened last night. Lieut. (now Capt.) Talbot United States Army, accompanied by Mr. R. S. Chew, arrived in Charleston and took quarters at the Charleston hotel.
He gave the authorities an official notification from the Lincoln government that Fort Sumter would be provisioned peaceably if practicable—forcibly if necessary. He did not visit Fort Sumter, (being I think denied that privilege,) but returned to Washington by the late train. So the war is at last declared.—*Charleston Mercury.—Observer, April 11th.*

(10.) April, 11th. I am informed by a member of the Cabinet that the steamers to Charleston carried no arms and no men, but only a supply of provisions for the government at Fort Sumter. I am also informed that Gov. Pickens was notified that such was the object of the steamer sent.—*Special to Petersburg Express.—Observer, April.15th.*

Note.—I think the above must be an error. These Steamers to Charleston, I think evidently went armed, with the intention of first trying to provision the fort peaceably and if that were resisted, they were then prepared to use force, but if I am not wrongly informed, the Lincoln government had informed the authorities at Charleston that no provisions nor any thing of the kind would be sent to Fort Sumter without first notifying the authorities at Charleston of the fact. This seems to have been done by Capt. Talbot and Mr. Chew.

(11.) Secession was spoken of in South Carolina, before it was known that Lincoln was elected, and when it was known in Charleston that he was elected, there was rejoicing over it. So they appeared to be seeking a cause for secession, rather than secession for a cause.— *March 14th.*

(12.) SPOILING FOR A FIGHT.

The Washington correspondent of the Charleston Mercury (himself at the safe distance of five hundred miles,) writes as follows to that paper.

Had a timely collision been had at Fort Sumter, Virginia and the rest might now have been with you. Inactivity is not always masterly.—*February 25th.*

(13.) COERCION.

A Kentuckian writes from Memphis to the Louisville Journal of the state of things there, and says, union men claim a majority. He closes his letter with the following significant incident:

It was but yesterday that I was questioned on the street in presence of several gentlemen as to the position that Kentucky would occupy, by two of the members of the late seceding convention of Mississippi, returning by this point to their homes on the Mississippi river. I answered that I thought Kentucky would adhere to the Union. The reply was, then we will, drag her out, and Maryland and Virginia and North Carolina and Tennessee all, if it be necessary.

How will you do so, was the demand?

Why all of these States have declared that coercion should not be used towards the seceding States. We will make a demonstration against Fort Sumter and Fort Pickens. At the first shot we will cry coercion and at the first cry of coercion we shall have all these States.—*February* 21*st*.

(14.) Gov. Gist has sent his last message to the Legislature, at its close he says:

The delay of the Convention for a single week to pass the ordinance of secession will have a blighting and chilling influence upon the action of the other Southern States, and the opponents of the movement will be encouraged to make another effort to rally their now disorganized and scattered forces to defeat our action and to stay our onward march.

Fabius conquered by delay, and there are those of his school, though with a more unworthy purpose, who, shrinking from an open and manly attack, use this vail to hide their deformities and from a masked battery discharge their missiles. But I trust they will strike the armor of truth and fall harmless at our feet, and that before the 25th of December no flag but the Palmetto will float over any part of South Carolina.— *Weekly Observer, December 17th,* 1860.

(15.) Do not distrust Virginia. As sure as to-morrows sun will rise upon us, just so sure will old Virginia be a member of this Southern Confederacy. And I will tell you gentlemen, what will put her in the Southern Confederation in less than an hour by Shrewsbury clock. Strike a blow. The very moment that blood is shed old Virginia will make common cause with her sisters of the South.—*Roger A. Pryor, April 15th.*

(16.) Judge John Robertson was sent as a commissioner to South Carolina.

After hearing Judge Robertson, the Legislature adopted among others the following resolutions:

Resolved unanimously, That the candor which is due to the long continued simpathy and respect which has subsisted between Virginia and South Carolina, induces this General Assembly to declare with frankness that they do not deem it advisable to initiate negociations when they have no desire or intention to promote the ultimate object in view, that object is declared in the resolutions of the legislature to be the procurement of new guarantees to the Constitution of the United States.

Resolved unanimously, That the separation of the State of South Carolina from the Federal Union is final, and she has no farther interest in the Constitution of the United States, and that the only appropriate negociations between her and the federal government are as to mutual relation as foreign States.—*February 4th.*

Note.—It will be recollected that Judge Robertson was sent as a commissioner by the State of Virginia to South Carolina for the purpose, it seems, of bringing about a reconciliation between the two sections by having new guarantees inserted in the Constitution—giving the South their rights, or in other words that she should not change her status or standing towards the general government, but wait and give time as it were, for obtaining these guaranties, when the above was the result.

(17.)   THE WAR POLICY.

It is not the general governmant that has proposed or desired coercion as is falsely pretended but the disunionists themselves. The administration has acted on the defensive. All the acts of war have proceeded from the capture of the forts, arsenals and navy yards in North and South Carolina, Georgia, Alabama, Mississippi, Louisiana and Florida, from those who fired on the stars and stripes in Charleston harbor, and those who are now investing forts Sumter and Pickens. They want war in the hope that all the South may thus be draged into disunion. In this spirit the Charleston Mercury publishes the following extract from a letter from Richmond, Virginia.

The only thing that can save us and unite the whole South is the capture of Fort Sumter before the end of this month. This will bring all Virginia to arms and the border States will follow her. Therefore, as much as I deplore bloodshed, I must advise prompt action.—*February 4th.*

(18) CHARLESTON MERCURY ON JOHN J. CRITTENDEN.

Mr. Crittenden is full of lamentations on the fall of the Union. In Congress and out of Congress—on the hustings and in the Senate—the Union is the theme of his laudation, and its destruction the burden of his woes, yet there is not a man alive—not Seward, nor Lincoln nor Greely—who has done more to dissolve the union than the Hon. John J. Crittenden.

He has never respected the people of the South, and therefore, has always counseled their submission to Northern insolence and aggression. He has all these lively hopes which spring from contempt. He has ever been, however unintentionally, one of the deadliest enemies of the South.—*February 4th.*

(19.) I have been engaged in this movement ever since I entered public life. We have carried the army of this union to its last resting place, and now we will drop the flag over its grave.—*Keitt f South Carolina.—January 28th.*

(20.) The Washington correspondent of the Richmond Dispatch uses the following language. Lincoln threatens war because he knows his hands are tied. War is not the thing we ought to fear. Peace is our destruction; war our salvation.—*March 21st.*

(21.) COLUMBIA, *November 13th.*

Mr. Keitt was serenaded last night at midnight, and made an exciting speech, urging prompt action:

He said, President Buchanan was pledged to secession, and would be held to it. South Carolina would shatter the accursed union. If she could accomplish its destruction in no other way she would throw her arms around the pillars of the Constitution and involve the States in a common ruin.—*November* 15*th*, 1860.

(22.) The secession of South Carolina is not an event of a day. It is not any thing produced by Lincoln's election, or by the non Intervention of the fugitive slave law. It has been a matter which has been gathering head for the last thirty years.—*Rhette of South Carolina, January* 28*th*.

(23.) There was, I think, another gentleman, a member of the South Carolina Convention, who said that he had been working for a dissolution of the Union for the last forty years. It not being convenient to refer to the paper giving an account of this, I think proper to with hold his name, but if you will examine the Observer file for the last of 1860 and first of 1861, you will be apt to bring him.

24.) It appears as soon as it was known that Lieut. James Jewet was about to leave Pensacola the State authorities of Florida ordered him to be arrested, and would not permit him to depart unless upon his parole of honor that he would never take up arms against the State of Florida. The document was truly drawn and presented to the Lieutenant, who accepted it as the only means of escape from prison. Without this document he could not have passed through the State.— *February* 7*th*.

By this it seems they anticipated war. But I think it would have been time enough to parole after hostilities had commenced.

(25.) The Richmond Enquirer advises the seizure of Washington City, with all the government buildings, with Fort Monroe at Old Point Comfort, and that the President should give up all the forts before March.— *December 24th.*

(26.) Governor Curtin announced to day to the Legislature that President Lincoln had written to him that he was informed of a design to attack Washington City. *April 11th.*

(27.) *Montgomery, Ala.*—President Davis and Secretary of War, Walker were serenaded at the Exchange hotel. The latter was called out and said that the Confederate flag would soon be waving over fort Sumter and from the Federal Copitol at Washington City, if the Independence of the Confederate States is not recognized, and hostilities continue.—*April 15th.*

(28.) It is seriously believed at Washington and the Northern cities that the Southern Confederacy is collecting an army of about 25,000 for a descent upon Washington City and the North Generally. It is said that Ben McCulloch has been making enlistments in Virginia for the same purpose.—*Observer file.*

(29.) WARLIKE THREATS AT MONTGOMERY

On Friday night after the news of the commencement of the bombardment had been received President Davis and Secretary Walker were serenaded. General Davis was too unwell to appear, and a speech was made by Secretary Walker, He said, no man could tell where the war this day commenced would end, but he would prophsy that the flag which now flaunts to the breeze here *would float over the dome of the old Capitol at Washington before the first of May.* Let them try Southern chivalry and test the extent of Southern resources, and it might float eventually in Boston over *Faneuil Hall itself.—Brother Jonathan.—New York, April 20th.*

(30.) Ex-President Filmore was for a convention to separate peaceably if the difficulties could not be adjusted.—*Observer file.*

(31.) There was a mob of 1,000 that tried to get hold on Wendell Phillips, the celebrated abolitionist, in Boston.—*December 27th.*

(32.) NEW YORK STATE CONVENTION.

They oppose coercion, favor Crittenden's compromise, exhort all men to unite with them in submitting that compromise to a vote of the people of the States; exhort all seceding States to refrain from acts of aggression or any course calculated to plunge the nation into civil war, and urge upon the non slave holding States to use their influence with their brethren South to that end.—*Albany, February, 1st, 1861.—Observer file.*

(33.) The fugitive slave law has times more than once caused free persons of color of the North to be sent into slavery.—*New York times.—Observer, January 10th.*

(34.) And if a man smite the eye of his servant or the eye of his maid that it perish; he shall let him go free for his eye's sake.

And if he smite out his man servants tooth or his maid servants tooth; he shall let him go free for his tooth's sake. Ex. xxi. 26, 27.

Then if a servant should have his liberty given him for the loss of an eye, or so small a member as a tooth, how much more should he have his liberty given him when he has been whiped for sooth almost to death. There has been almost every degree of punishment inflicted in these Southern States. Some have been whiped until it has caused their death; others so as to be on the verge of death; and others so as to be bed-ridden for several weeks. These cases though, as elsewhere mentioned, are exceeding rare; and I do not wish to create the impression that they are, so far as my knowledge goes, any thing else but very rare, being scarcely witnessed in a life time in this section.

The suffering caused by the loss of an eye, or so small a member as a tooth, must be small in comparison to what is suffered in one of those brutish whippings. Whilst I consider such treatment as unnecessary to enforce obedience, I look upon it as savage and inhuman, unbecoming a civilized nation. I therefore think there should be laws passed such as would insure their general good treatment.

It may be argued that laws have already been passed in most if not all of the slave States respecting the treatment of servants; so there have been. But is there much more attention paid to these laws than if they had not been passed? Is it not very rarely, almost never I might say, that we hear of any one being reported for mistreatment of his servants, whereas instances of mistreatment do some times take place. But until a law is passed to fine heavily our Sheriffs, Magistrates and even private citizens, if they even know of such an instance of mistreatment and fail to report it, we need not expect to see the requisitions of such a law carried out. Notwithstanding such may be on the several statute books of all the slave States, there will be but little more attention paid to them than if they were not there, without some such a provision as has been mentioned. But by having a law that the owner should forfeit the freedom of his servant mistreated, and then fined about $1,000 into the bargain, one half to the informer, the other half to the State, I think the evil could be effectually broken up.

These laws passed, we might then I think, expect soon to see these few exceptions to good treatment effectually done away with.

(35.) And if thy brother that dwelleth by thee be waxen poor and be sold unto thee, thou shall not compel him to serve as a bond servant.

But as a hired servant, and as a sojourner, he shall be with thee, and shall serve thee unto the year of jubilee:

And then shall he depart from thee, both he and his children with him, and shall return unto his own family, and unto the possession of his fathers shall he return.

For they are my servants which I brought forth out of the land of Egypt; they shall not be sold as bondmen. Thou shalt not rule over him with rigor, but shalt fear thy God.

Both thy bondmen, and thy bondmaids, which thou shalt have, shall be of the heathen that are round about you; of them shall ye buy bondmen and bondmaids.

Moreover of the children of strangers that do sojourn among you, of them shall ye buy, and of their families that are with you, which they begat in your land; and they shall be your possession.

And ye shall take them as an inheritance for your children after you, to inherit them for a possession; they shall be your bondmen forever; but over your brethren the children of Israel, ye shall not rule one over another with rigor. Lev. xxv. 39—46.

(36.) Thou shalt not deliver unto his master the servant which is escaped from his master unto thee. Deut. xxiii. 15.

(37.) Among other laws that Lycurgus introduced

into Sparta was one, that a man's daughters should inherit no part of their father's estate, but that it should be divided equally among his sons. Being called upon to explain the object of this curious law, he said: "The young men in making matches would not then be choosing for property, but would go for worth and merit." It would also seem to tend to prevent the sexes from leading lives of the unnatural state of celibacy, for they frequently keep picking and choosing for property, until they pick through and get nobody.

(38.) The progress of the negro race in the Slave States is remarkable and unexampeled. At the year of our independence, there were in all of the thirteen origional States, composing the then Federal Union, but little more than 600,000 slaves—twelve of these being slave States. . Of those, seven became afterward free States, leaving out of the thirteen, to the South, but five. Yet there is at the South to-day a slave population of between four-and-a-half and five millions of slaves; happier and better cared for in physicial and spiritual relation, than any other equal numbers of industrial classes upon the face of the globe. Nay, but the slaves are generally in every element of utility, respectability, and refinement, far in advance of the free negroes of the slave States even. "As to a free negro hiring himself out for plantation labor," writes Mr. Lewis, seventeen years before the act of British emancipation, "no instance of such a thing was ever known in Jamaica; and probably no price, however great, would be considered by them as a sufficient temptation." And the same is true of the free negro everywhere. In 1839, one year after the act of emancipation, the exportation of sugar from the island of Jamaica had fallen off 8,460 hogsheads, while the exportation of coffee, in the same year, had decreased 38,554 hundreds weight—almost one-third of the whole amount of the preceding year. Between 1846 and 1853, there were *one hundred and sixty-eight sugar estates* wholly abandoned, and sixty-three partially— valued thee years after the emancipation at nearly eight and a half millions of dollars. Of coffee plantations, there were twenty partially, and two hundred and twenty-three completely, deserted;—valued in the same year at $2,500,000; while of grazing farms, there were one hundred and thirty two totally or partially forsaken valued at about a million and a half of dollars—making a grand total, in seven years, of over six hundred estates, relinquished to barbarism and decay, and valued forty years ago at nearly $13,000,000. *Now*, according to John Bigelow, one of the editors of the New York *Evening Post*, "the finest land in the world may be had at any price and almost for the asking. Labor receives no compensation; and the product of labor does not seem to know how to find the way to market." Estates, which once were worth $2,000 per annum, do not now yield the value of the cultivation. The busy hum of the mills and machinery of capitalists are silenced in Jamaica. The free negroes, in sloth and idleness, bask in the sunshine, upon what were formely the plantations of their masters. While the intrepid Englishman is sacrificing his life beneath a burning sun, the negro, lives by stealing, or carrying away as a matter of course the yams which grow spontaneously upon the plantations of the former. Where were formerly the race-course and the theatre—where the city rose in pride, and happy faces thronged the market-place—there are to-day ruin and desolation; rats and negroes disputing their respective claims to squatter sovereignty, and nettles and ivy ornamenting the site of public buildings.

Even British Guiana—once the garden of gardens—has become a wild forest again—swamps and wildbeasts have taken the place of cultivation and civilized man. All along the bank of the Demarara river, before emancipation blossoming like the rose and covered with plaintains and coffee, there are now misery, desolation, broken bridges, and impassible roads. Essequibo, and its once famous Arabian coast, formerly the boast of British colonists, is now almost a desert waste. And the fate of Berbice is no better. Of its 18,000 black inhabitants, twelve thousand have degenerated to a condition of pure savagism, and withdrawn from all industrial pursuits in ignorence and idleness. In 1829, the district on the west bank of the Berbice river, gave employment to nearly four thousand slaves; whereas there are hardly five hundred persons employed there now. The whole is rapidly becoming one vast swamp; and, to use the language of the historian, Alision: "*the negroes, who in a state of slavery were comfortable and prosperous beyond any peasantry in the world, and rapidly approaching the condition of the most opulent serfs in Europe, have been by the act of emancipation irretrievably consigned to barbarism.*"

The same may be said of Hayti, once the pride of the ocean, now a political curse and social ulcer, with the monstrous tragedy of which the reader cannot be unacquainted. Robespierre, Danton, Brissot, and other bloodhounds and incarnate devils, of the French Revolution, calling themselves *Amis des Nois*, and anticipating the Beechers, Sewards, Garrisons, Phillipses, and Parkers, of the North, stimulated the negroes of this unfortunate Island into a servile and barbarous insurrection. The atrocities which ensued are without a parallel in the most diabolical annals of crime. "The victorious slaves," says Alison in his "History of Europe,"—"marched with spiked infants on their spears instead of colors, and sawed assunder the male prisoners. And when this demonical work of unutterable brutality,in the drama of Haytien "liberty" was completed—what followed? The sugar exported from this Island in the year 1789 amounted to 672,000,000 pounds. In 1806, seventeen years after, the exportation had fallen to 47,516,531 pounds. Nineteen years later, in 1825, the exportation of sugar from Hayti was 2,020 pounds, and in seven years more it had entirely ceased! Thus by giving freedom to Haytien negroes, in the short space of forty-three years, humanity and civilization, were deprived, in the aggregate, of 28,896,000,000 pounds of sugar ond the Queen-Island of the seas relinquished to barbarism, desolation, brutal licentiousness, and crime in every hideous form. In a condition of slavery, the the negro may prove himself to be a most useful interesting, and affectionate animal; but he will not work without a master. The experiment of Joshua R. Giddings—the most generous and sincere of all American abolitionists—exemplifies this. He had a large tract of land settled by negroes, upon each of whom he bestowed a portion of it, with all of the implements necessary to the farmer. In a few years the village was deserted, the land remained waste and uncultivated, and Mr. Giddings was constrained to confess that his black Eutopia was but a fond and idle dream.—*Cause and Contrast, pp.* 87–91.

Note To prove farther that the Blacks that are in servitude are in a happier and better condition than their free brethren North or South are in I refer to the following.
In 1800 there were in the United States 1,087,359,

free blacks are only 893,041 slaves. In 1851, the slave population of the Southern States was 3,204,287, and the free black population of the whole United States was only 434,495 and of these there resided over half in the Slave States. Thus it seems while the slave population has been increasing without scarcely a parcill in history, the free black has been decreasing as fast for it. This does not argue well in favor of emancipation.

(39.) The husbandman that laboreth must first be partaker of the fruits. ii Tim. ii. 6.

Although it does not mention servants in the above text I think it is evedint that,if the Husbandman that laboreth should receive of the first fruits,the servant that laboreth should be allowed to partake of at least the common stock.

(40.) People being so ready to engage in wars and battles reminds me of a piece that I was once reading which I will here relate.

There were once two soldiers that had a falling out. One sent the other a challenge to fight a duel. The one challenged declined accepting. The other one taunted him with the name coward. The soldies also soon took a part in it and thinking that the man that shows fight under any and every occasion is the man they too taunted this other gentleman with the name, coward. So he soon came to be look upon and pointed at by all as a coward. At last this epithet became rather familiar to our friedd. So one evening whilst he was in a room with a good many of his fellow soldiers upon some of them taunting him again with his rather familiar name hesays to them: Gentlemen I will see who of you will dare true bravery. So saying ho pulled out a hand grenade and held the fuse to a candle until it had lighted; he then threw it on the floor. There was immediately a general stampede for the door, and in their hurry to get out a good many were precipated and knocked down ; so there was for awhile at the door a complete mass of crawling flesh about waist deep. The door though was after awhile cleared and they all out and gone. Our friend still stood over the grenade with his arms folded. At last hearing the explosion they ran in expecting to find him torn in pieces ; but they found him there with his arms still folded safe and sound. He remarked that if he risked his life, he wished it to be where there was a prospect of its doing some good, such as in defense of his country when wrongly assailed, or in personal defense. But as for fighting duels he did not desire thus needlessly to kill nor to be killed. After this they did not taunt him any more as being a coward.

There is a moral in the above to which I wish to call the attention of the reader. You have doubtless noticed that it is not always the man that talks the most and makes the the greatest display with words that is always the most truly brave; though they frequently do much harm by a display of their malignant dispositions, as small dogs, which are more quarrelsome, frequently put larger ones to fighting.

But were I going to pick for a truly brave man, one that combines bravery with prudence, I would take one that says but little of his plans and purposes until it comes time to act. When it thus becomes necessary for him to act, he does so with his whole soul and energy

There is another reason why people should avoid going to war as much as possible—they are apt to grow fond of it and thus become schooled and nurtured in an evil as it were. Wars I think in this way tend to demoralize man, and to make him more atrocious and wicked than he otherwise would be. This may be likened unto a surgeon doctor in his first practice. At first he feels great timidity and fear in his surgical operations, but by practice he soon gets so that he can amputate a limb without feeling any of this timidity whatever; so of wars. A man by being frequently in battles gets use to seeing the dead, and sometimes, I presume, even a fondness is formed for the novelties of the battle field. From the fact that man thus becomes hardened and demoralized is, I think, of itself, sufficient to teach us that wars should be avoided as much as possible.

I will endeavor to make my position a little plainer by the following comparison; though somewhat novel it will probably answer for an illustration. The Rattle snake is probably the most deadly and fatal of any of the reptile tribe, with which man has to contend, yet he is not the first to resort to violence. He will first give you warning with one twitch of his rattle; if you still intrude you may then expect a deadly wound. Some of the smaller reptiles would have you bitten two or three times before the rattle snake strikes once, but when he does strike, he makes up for all. He appears to be slow to anger. Even here, among the reptiles, man is taught a lesson—be slow to anger. We should wait until justice fully demands that we should strike a blow; we may then expect it to be more effective.

(41)   HENRY CLAY ON SECESSION.

He said, I have been asked when I would consent to give up this Union. I answer never, never, never! and I warn you now my countrymen if as things seem to tend, this country shall be divided into a union and disunion party, I here now, no matter who compose that party, declare myself a member of the Union party. Whether it be a Whig or a Democrat that belongs to the party of the union, there I subscribe my name, there I unite my heart and hand with that party.

Extract of a speech delivered in Bowling Green in 1850.

I will only ask the question if the old patriot was with us to-day which side do you think he would be on?

CONTENTS.

	PAGE
I.	
THE SECTIONAL TROUBLES.	5
II.	
SECESSION OF SOUTH CAROLINA.	12
III.	
TAKING OF FORT SUMTER.	17
IV.	
FURTHER PARTICULARS.	25
V.	
PRESIDENT LINCOLN ISSUES HIS PROCLAMATION CALLING FOR 75,000 TROOPS.	29
VI.	
LETTERS OF MARQUE ISSUED.	34
VII.	
PERSONAL LIBERTY BILLS.	35
VIII.	
TREATMENT OF SERVANTS.	40
IX.	
TREATMENT OF SERVANTS—*Continued*.	47
X.	
BLOCKADE ESTABLISHED.	49
XI.	
OUR GOVERNMENT AS COMPARED WITH OTHERS.	66

XII.
Further Comparison. - - - - 72
XIII.
Plan of Adjustment. - - - 78
XIV.
Plan of Adjustment—*Continued.* With an argument that the righteous should rule. - 89
XV.
Sudden call of God and Profession of Religion. 97
XVI.
Further Account. - - - - 120
XVII.
General Review. - - - - 125
XVIII.
Conclusion. - - - - - 136

ERRATA.

Numerous typographical errors have doubtless been noticed in the foregoing and particularly in the first four forms, or first ninety-six pages of the book. The great haste with which we have frequently gone to press, together with my own inexperience, being my first attempt at correcting a proof sheet, will, I hope, be considered a sufficient apology for these errors; some of the principal of which I will here notice:

For						
For	It,	page	10	line	15	read I.
"	allawance,	"	8	"	14	" allowance.
"	meecy,	"	8	"	29	" mercy.
"	case,	"	12	"	1	" cause.
"	electorial,	"	14	"	4	" electoral.
"	peaceable,	"	18	"	26	" peaceably.
"	rought,	"	42	"	12	" rough.
"	then,	"	48	"	14	" there.
"	except,	"	48	"	30	" expect.
"	somebohy,	"	52	"	34	" somebody.
"	off,	"	55	"	29	" of.
"	prop,	"	65	"	35	" drop.
"	unimployed,	"	67	"	12	" unemployed.
"	unrivaleed,	"	69	"	4	" unrivaled.
"	presperity,	"	69	"	4	" prosperity.
"	recources,	"	69	"	8	" resources.
"	stricture,	"	69	"	28	" structure.
"	conditions,	"	80	"	14	" condition.
"	obsticable,	"	80	"	24	" obsticle.
"	quiting,	"	93	"	23	" quitting.
"	nature,	"	71	"	5	" nature.
"	had,	"	112	"	3	" has.
"	againgt,	"	145	"	33	"

www.ingramcontent.com/pod-product-compliance
Lightning Source LLC
Chambersburg PA
CBHW020252170426
43202CB00008B/336